PUBLIC
PLACES

The Nearby History Series
David E. Kyvig, *Series Editor*
Myron A. Marty, *Consulting Editor*

Public Places

Exploring Their History

Gerald A. Danzer

The American Association for State and Local History
Nashville, Tennessee

Library of Congress Cataloging in Publication Data

Danzer, Gerald A.
  Public places

  (The Nearby history series; 3)
  Bibliography
  Includes index
  1. Public history—United States. 2. United States—History, Local. 3. Local history. 4. Historic sites—United States. I. Title. II. Series.
  E180.D36   1987   973   87-19508
  ISBN 0-910050-88-0

Cover design by Gillian Murrey

Contents

Editors' Introduction

COMMUNITIES WITHOUT AN UNDERSTANDING OF THEIR pasts resemble people suffering from amnesia, unable to remember from where they came, how they responded to needs or challenges, from whence they drew affection and support, or opposition, and where they intended to go. History, the contemplation and evaluation of the past, serves society much as memory serves the individual in identifying circumstances, providing a guide to appropriate behavior, and offering a standard of comparison across time and situation. In this sense, history is far more than a remembrance of things past, though it certainly includes that. History represents a means of coming to terms with the past, of developing an awareness of previous influences, current conditions, and future possibilities. Just as memory helps the individual avoid repeating the same discoveries, behaviors, and mistakes, historical knowledge helps a community avoid starting at the beginning each time it addresses an issue.

History, in addition to being useful, is accessible. Any literate person can master and pursue most historical research techniques as well as understand and critically evaluate historical explanations. Furthermore, history is interesting. Whether reading other people's mail, understanding how ordinary people lived their everyday lives at other times and in other places, or assessing how institutions rose or decayed, the individual studying history constantly finds exciting opportunities to learn about the human condition.

All of these values of history hold as true for the nearby world as for the larger sphere. English historian H. P. R. Finberg considered "the family, the local community, the national state, and the supra-national society as a series of concentric circles." He observed, "Each requires to be studied with constant reference to the one outside it; but the inner rings are not the less perfect circles for being wholly surrounded and enclosed by the outer." In fact, understanding the history of the world close at hand is of great value, for it is this history that shapes the circumstances we must deal with directly and constantly.

In 1982, we wrote a book that asserted the importance of taking a look at the history of the close-at-hand world and attempted to provide assistance in so doing. *Nearby History: Exploring the Past around You* was by design merely an introduction to a broad and complex topic. The book sought to raise questions for consideration, to point out the sorts of materials that exist for historical research, to suggest generally how they might be used, and to indicate some of the published works on nearby historical topics that might offer useful models or comparisons. *Nearby History* was predicated on the belief that useful inquiry into the nearby past was not an undertaking for academic professionals alone but could be pursued in a worthwhile fashion by any interested student or out-of-school adult. We intended to stir interest and to indicate how local concerns could comfortably mesh with sophisticated historical thinking.

Growing interest in the subjects and objectives addressed in *Nearby History* has persuaded us that a need exists for a series of books focused on specific aspects of the close-at-hand world. Particular issues and institutions in the community deserving historical consideration pose individual problems of research and analysis. Schools, homes, public places, and churches are among the nearby world's features that deserve to be addressed historically, each in its own way. The volumes in the "Nearby History" series will give outstanding specialists in these areas the opportunity to offer guidance and insight to readers engaged in their own local investigations.

Public Places: Exploring Their History by Gerald A. Danzer represents a departure from previous "Nearby History" series volumes on schools and homes. Instead of focusing on a single institution, this book looks at a broad category of spaces and places within the community, those that are generally accessible to residents and visitors as opposed to those that are private or somehow restricted. In public places, private lives intersect; the members of a community find common ground. Danzer offers a thoughtful guide to investigating the history of places intended for human encounters: monuments for social ceremony and remembrance; buildings for commerce, culture, and government; parks and open spaces for recreation and respite; and even streets, which serve as meeting sites as well as thoroughfares. In addition, Danzer suggests how the consideration of initial plans for a community and the subsequent development of particular places can lead to an understanding of the community as a whole, its evolution, its interactions, and its character. After discussing ways of thinking about a community's public places, he provides some specific and practical advice on nearby history research and presentation in a series of helpful appendices.

Danzer's insightful way of looking at communities aided us when we were writing *Nearby History*. It has also assisted students and teachers engaged in local history undertakings at the Chicago Historical Society, the Chicago Metro History Fair, the Newberry Library, and the University of Illinois at Chicago. We believe that, as set forth here, his approach will prove useful to others interested in the history of the nearby world, whether they are venturing into this fascinating subject for the first time or are looking for fresh insights on a seemingly familiar topic.

DAVID E. KYVIG, Series Editor
MYRON A. MARTY, Consulting Editor

Acknowledgments

I HAVE BEEN THINKING ABOUT NEARBY HISTORY FOR more than a decade. During this time, three public places have been regular stops on my beat: the Chicago Historical Society, the Newberry Library, and the University of Illinois at Chicago. It was at the second institution that I came to know and respect the approach to nearby history represented by the work of David Kyvig and Myron Marty. Harold Skramstad, Ellsworth Brown, Richard Brown, David Buisseret, and Arthur Anderson at the society and the library have found ways to encourage my work over the years. My colleagues at the university have kept me alert through mutual discussions of our work. In particular, I owe large intellectual debts to Perry Duis, Mel Holli, Richard Jensen, Burt Bledstein, Al Larson, and Larry McBride.

David Wilson graciously located the post cards used in chapter 4 among the treasures of his splendid collection. The rest of the illustrations are either from my personal hoard of books, from the library of the University of Illinois at Chicago, or from materials produced by the Chicago Neighborhood History Project. Magdalene, my wife, not only read the entire manuscript and critiqued some earlier versions, but has also accompanied me on many·side trips. As we looked at many a public square and dozens of old buildings, she wisely suggested when it was time to stay and when it was time to go. Thanks again, Honey.

GERALD A. DANZER

Preface

THIS BOOK IS ABOUT THE PUBLIC ASPECTS OF OUR nearby history, those buildings and places that pertain to the life of the people as a whole. When you think about it, almost all spaces and places have public dimensions. Whether you are interested in the history of a street or a town, of a church or a school, of a house or a building, you will need to consider its public aspects. People, after all, develop their potential as human beings in social groups. This book's purpose is to consider the public dimension of the local environment, to see that environment as a product of historical forces, and, finally to contemplate the relationship of individual members of a community to the places where they encounter each other.

Why should we study public places? What does a knowledge of their history and function contribute to our understanding of the world? How does nearby history help us become more complete human beings? The connection between an appreciation of public places and citizenship is not hard to perceive:

It is small things remembered, the little corners of the land, the houses, the people that each one loves. We love our country because there was a little tree on a hill, and grass thereon, and a sweet valley below; because the hurdy-gurdy man came along on a sunny morning in a city street; because a beach or a farm or a lane or a house that might not seem much to others was once, for each of us, made of magic.

These comments by an editorialist in the *New York Times* some years ago (quoted in Rudolph Flesch, *How to Write, Speak, and Think More Effectively* [New York: Harper, 1960], pp. 60-61) go a long way toward answering our questions, but they do not tell the whole story. Personal experiences build memories, which transform ordinary landscapes into magical places. But there are also communal memories, which turn public places into civic pageants. And then there are facilities that make up the silent infrastructure of a community, those constructions that make possible individual adventures.

Our daily activities take place on a stage we have inherited from the past. Few communities are built from scratch at one time. Most of us are like hermit crabs using the streets and buildings built by other generations and left behind for us to adapt for our purposes and to pass on to the next generation. To realize this aspect of our existence is to gain a civic education.

Many people have studied, in a formal way, the interaction between places and social behavior. While it would certainly be instructive to follow these discussions in the scholarly literature, our purpose is much more focused. This book is addressed to people interested in nearby history, to those who like to look around their own communities with understanding, and to those inquisitive folks who, for one reason or another, want to learn about the places they encounter. How can sensitivity to the public aspects of communities inform their attempts to understand nearby history? How can this book be of help? In four ways, I think.

First, throughout these pages a basic theme is played in a variety of ways: individual people, places, and events can be understood only in the context of the community. Without public places, there can be no civic life, no community, no way of telling who we are, where we have been, or where we are going. It will take several chapters to explore the ramifications of public places, but there is no better way to develop the power of nearby history to meet contemporary needs.

Second, as this book explores public places, it introduces readers to a variety of historical materials. Each of the first five chapters highlights one type of primary source: speeches, promotional pamphlets, maps, post card views, and annual reports. These are the kinds of documents usually available for local history projects. There is nothing complicated in how historians use them, but their explanatory powers are often overlooked. By consciously focusing on one type of source in each chapter, the text offers a model for others to use.

The third way this book can help those engaged in local history is to suggest some avenues of interpretation. Our central purpose is to see, in the past around us, some broader significance. It is this quest for meaning that makes one a historian. It is also difficult to teach, to reduce to a plan in a manual of instruction. But each chapter demonstrates the range of possibilities by offering a list of suggestions for the interpretation of public space. There is some overlapping of suggestions from chapter to chapter, and several ideas are useful only for unusual topics, but these discussions are the heart of the book. If local historians neglect the push for broader understanding, their work becomes subject to serious criticism. Indeed the author, the editors, and the publisher of this volume will be richly rewarded if readers come away from the book not only with some knowledge about public places but also with some ideas about interpreting them.

The fourth means by which this book seeks to help people interested in nearby history is to provide them with some suggestions for further reading. A brief bibliographical section concludes each chapter. The lists are selective, indicating the range of available materials and pointing to a dozen or so key works that the reader may turn to if he or she wishes to extend the discussion started in the chapter. Most of these books and articles are readily available through local libraries. Others will take some effort to locate, usually being found only at larger university or public libraries. Every work cited can be supplied through interlibrary loan or by photocopy. For this reason specific pages and chapters are often suggested as being most germane to the topic at hand.

The book's organization is very simple. It divides public places into five categories and devotes a chapter to each one. It starts with monuments, those structures or places supplying a symbol of the community to residents and outsiders alike. Chapter 2 focuses on buildings, those owned by the people as a whole and those owned by individuals but having a public profile nonetheless. The third chapter is the most abstract and will demand the closest attention. It suggests that they very plan of a community gives every specific part a public aspect. Each lot or building is one piece of the whole community. Historians have often overlooked the plan of a community as a whole, and chapter 3 seeks to redress the oversight.

The next two chapters bring us back to more familiar ground. Chapter 4 discusses streets and roads; chapter 5 centers on parks and open spaces. A concluding chapter shows the reader how to put all of these public places together into a model for analyzing his or her own town. It inventories the types of public places in any community and suggests some general outlines for their history. At that point, readers may want to get going on their own projects and adventures. Several appendices provide specific guidance in doing so.

·1·

Monuments

WHAT IS THE NATURE OF PUBLIC PLACES, AND HOW DO they function? What is the relationship between public places and private places? How do these areas relate to the past? Why does a site need a history to become a public place? One way to begin constructing answers to these questions is to sort public places into several different categories. Such an approach might divide them into monuments, buildings, community plans, streets, and open spaces. A good place to start is with monuments.

Monuments, in a utilitarian sense, seem to be the least important of the various types of public places; yet they clearly illuminate the essential public element of a place—that is, the connecting of an individual person with a group and, in the process, providing him or her with an identity and a model for proper behavior. Monuments tell us who we are, inform us where we came from, list the ideals we should honor, and suggest the goals toward which we should strive. They do so by reminding us of some person or event from the past, as the origin of word, derived from the Latin verb, "to remind," suggests.

Lots of things can become monuments—tombs, trees, buildings, or rusty cannons, for example—but monuments can also be specifically designed to instruct the future. In each case, they have both a horizontal and a vertical dimension—that is, they serve as rallying points for group solidarity at one point in time, binding a community together horizontally, but also vertically connecting the present generation with a heroic past and a fulfilling destiny.

Builders of monuments consciously strive to keep alive memories from the collective past for the guidance of their contemporaries, but they also aim to carry their message to future generations. Because people in every

1

period believe they will be remembered by the monuments they erect, they strive for edifices not only equal to the glorious people and events they commemorate, but also worthy of representing the current society to future generations.

The high calling, the almost sacred purpose of monuments, usually has necessitated a formal dedication ceremony during which these sites were set apart from the ordinary lands of a community. Every form of public place, whether street or square, water works or courthouse, shares this characteristic. If a structure or site is dedicated with a special civic ceremony, it almost always has the attributes of a public place.

Records of the dedication ceremony often recall the chain of events leading from the original idea for a monument to its formal unveiling. The speeches given at various ceremonies accompanying the construction help the historian develop a context in which a monument can be appreciated. A brief look at the dedication of one of our nation's most celebrated monuments will clarify some basic points about public places in general and monuments in particular.

The Washington Monument

The Washington National Monument was dedicated with appropriate ceremonies on February 21, 1885. The dedication marked the end of a process dating back to December 19, 1799, the day after George Washington was buried at Mt. Vernon. On that day, John Marshall, then a member of Congress from Virginia, proposed that a committee be formed to find a way to remember the citizen, who, in Marshall's fitting phrase, was "first in war, first in peace, and first in the hearts of his countrymen." Lack of agreement on the nature and the site for a national commemorative structure delayed progress on the effort until 1833. Then some private citizens took matters into their own hands and established the Washington National Monument Society. Chief Justice Marshall, seventy-eight years old at the time, was elected its president. After several years, the group raised enough funds to commission an architectural design, and finally, on July 4, 1848, the cornerstone was laid.

Robert C. Winthrop of Massachusetts, the speaker of the House of Representatives, gave the oration at the laying of the cornerstone. The raising of the monumental shaft then proceeded year by year. Funds ran out around 1856 when the obelisk had reached a height of 156 feet. The work stopped during the Civil War and was not taken up again until 1876 when Congress took over the project, enlarged the foundation, and completed "the grandest monumental column ever erected in any age of the world." Thus the stage was set for a festive dedication on the eve of Washington's birthday in 1885 (fig. 1-1).

The aged Winthrop was invited to give the major oration once again. Although too infirm to attend the ceremony in person, he did compose a fitting piece that still serves as an excellent introduction to the monument. It was important for Winthrop to participate—his contribution was an element of continuity in the thirty-seven long years between the laying of the cornerstone and placement of the capstone. Winthrop's role in 1885 made vivid the vertical function of monuments, that of connecting generations across time.

The monument was simplified during the years of construction from the original plan of Robert Mills, whose design had called for an elaborate colonnade at the base of the column. The simple obelisk form had been used in the Bunker Hill Monument in 1825 and received widespread approval

GROUNDS OF THE DEPARTMENT OF AGRICULTURE AND MONUMENT SQUARE.

Fig. 1-1. The Washington Monument in 1885. The site of the Washington Monument was intentionally kept free of buildings to emphasize the monument's great height. The view westward from the Capitol looked down the mall to the obelisk, with the tidal flats and the Potomac River beyond. In the distance, the hills of Virginia reminded people of the westward sweep of the nation. From Stilson Hutchins and Joseph West Moore's, *The National Capital: Past and Present*, (1885).

for its harmonious blending of "durability, simplicity, and grandeur." In both cases, the proportions from antiquity were carefully followed, but the height of the Washington Monument increased until it pushed the limits of contemporaneous engineering. In contrast to the monuments of Egypt, which were usually cut in the quarry from a single stone, the American edifices were composed of many pieces. The interior of the Washington Monument used stones from every state and territory and from many foreign nations as well. The variety of blocks, massed together in one consolidated structure, typified the nation as a whole. The monument "will ever be an instructive type of the National strength," Winthrop declared, "which can only be secured by the union of many in one."

The simplicity of the colossal shaft was good, the orator observed, because there would be "ample opportunity for the display of decorative art" throughout the land. "The streets and squares of this city and of all our great cities are wide open for statues and architectural memorials." Here the flowering of the decorative arts and the development of modern designs could proceed without restraint. The connection between national and local history was then underscored: "Such monuments are everywhere welcomed and honored."

The supporting cast of local monuments would need inscriptions to instruct the citizens, but Washington's monument was blank, severe in its simplicity. No inscriptions, Winthrop observed, were ever likely to be engraved on it, for the lessons and precepts of the founding father "will come blazing forth in letters of living light" out of the memory of every patriotic citizen. Hence, Winthrop concluded, it was the responsibility of those legislators assembled to supply the rising generation "with the means of that Universal Education which is the crying want of our land, and without which any intelligent and successful Free Government is impossible." The monument's inscription would be supplied from the schoolbooks of American democracy.

Our story could go on to consider other speeches given on that chilly winter's day. The brief comments by President Chester Arthur on the legacy of Washington would be a good place to turn to next in the discussion, but our account has gone far enough to begin listing a few themes for the interpretation of any monument or public place.

Suggestions for Interpretation

History. Every monument has a history. Figure 1-2 diagrams the process of monument building from the inception of a project through its design and construction and on to its subsequent use. When researching the history of a monument, the historian will want to look for materials that document each stage of its life. The full story is often cut short by projects that, at one stage or another, faltered, as the Washington National Monument languished in Congress from 1799, the date of the first legislation, until 1833 when the private committee was formed to get the project moving. This group, in turn, ran out of energy at the funding stage and could only get the monument one-fourth of the way built. At several points in the early stages of development, the effort faced competition from other groups seeking to erect similar monuments at different sites and in different styles.

Design. The designs submitted for a monument, the one subsequently chosen, and the adaptations of the design are all important to the historian. Thus our second rubric, "design," should not be limited to the plan that was executed. It is instructive to see how the original design of Robert Mills for the Washington Monument was simplified, first, out of economic necessity and, in the end, out of national choice. No one after 1885 seriously proposed "finishing" the monument by adding the Greek-styled circular pantheon at the base. Such a classical ornament might have been more in character with the rest of the architecture in the capital city, but the desire for an Egyptian-style monument went back to the 1799 Congressional resolution, which specified a pyramid. The reference to Pharaonic Egypt rather than democratic Greece or republican Rome certainly raises some questions, as does the ultimate decision to follow Old World models for a New World hero. Winthrop, by the way, addressed both of these concerns in his 1885 oration.

Materials. The choice of materials to be used for the structure was, of course, directly related to the design. An important question, however, is whether the building committee or sponsoring group stipulated that the materials should be local, brought from some distance, or even imported. The Washington Monument was faced with local Maryland marble, but the harder granite required for the interior supporting stones had to be shipped from New England. Special stones were sent by a variety of governments and institu-

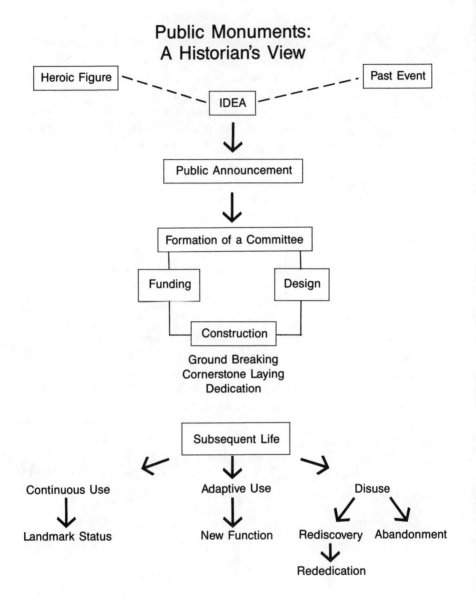

Public Monuments:
A Historian's View

Heroic Figure - - - - - - - - - - - - - Past Event

IDEA

Public Announcement

Formation of a Committee

Funding   Design

Construction

Ground Breaking
Cornerstone Laying
Dedication

Subsequent Life

Continuous Use   Adaptive Use   Disuse

Landmark Status   New Function   Rediscovery   Abandonment

Rededication

Fig. 1-2

tions to be included in the interior. Some are inscribed "The Swiss Free Confederation," "Cherokee Nation," "Templars of Honor and Temperance, New York," and so on. One of the stones with the most explanatory power was never put in the structure. A block of African marble from the Temple of Concord in Rome was sent by the pope with the simple inscription, "Rome to America." A "fanatical minister" made the gift an issue, and in 1854, at the time of the Know-Nothing movement, the stone was stolen from a warehouse and presumably dropped into the Potomac River.

Site. The site chosen for a monument and its niche in the cityscape also are important to the historian. A statue of George Washington had been ordered by Congress under the Articles of Confederation as early as 1783, but the legislators did not know where to put it. Pierre L'Enfant's plan, prepared in 1791, for the seat of government specified a variety of details. The first one, marked with an A on L'Enfant's map, is for "the equestrian figure of George Washington, a monument voted in 1783 by the late Continental Congress." The site was at the end the plan's "Grand Avenue" leading westward from the Capitol to a point where it intersected with a line due south from the president's house. One could argue that the site for the Washington Monument was the main pivot around which the federal city was designed.

The site of a building refers to the land on which it is built, and any parcel of real estate is defined by its place in the comprehensive plan of the community. To evaluate any particular site, one needs to look at a map of the entire community. Another aspect related to the site, and to the design, is how the elevation of the monument fits into the overall skyline of the city or the facade formed by the buildings in the area. The Washington Monument stood alone on its site, towering far above all the other buildings in the city, the nation, and, indeed, in the history of the world (fig. 1-3).

In his dedication oration, Winthrop commented that the "soaring shaft, rising high above trees and spires and domes and all the smoke and stir of earth" reflected Washington's vision that "rose above sectional prejudices and party politics and personal interests—overtopping and dominating all its surroundings, gleaming and glistening out at every vista as far as human sight can reach, arresting and riveting the eye at every turn, while it shoots triumphantly to the skies."

In 1885, the Washington Monument was indeed the tallest structure the world had ever seen. It soon lost that distinction when the Eiffel Tower

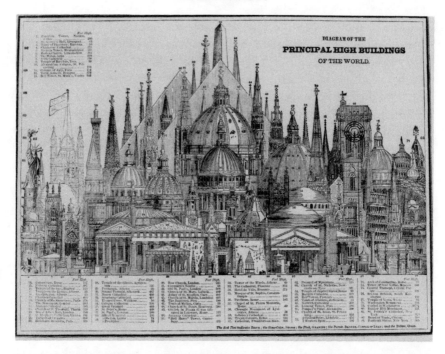

Fig. 1-3. "Diagram of the Principal High Buildings of the World." Pages like this one appeared in many popular atlases published in the late nineteenth century. Until 1885, the monuments of the Old World dominated the heights. The completion of the Washington Monument seemed to mark the arrival of the United States as a leader in world civilization. From *Chandler's New and Complete Family Atlas of the World* (Rockford, Ill.: Chandler Bros., 1896).

was completed in 1889. In the United States, however, the shaft overlooking the Potomac exceeded the height of all the early skyscrapers in Chicago and New York. Not until 1908, when the Singer Building was erected in New York City, was the Washington Monument exceeded in height by an American structure. Today the monument remains the tallest masonry construction ever built and the highest edifice in the national capital where the height of buildings is now restricted by law.

Inscriptions. The fifth window to the historical interpretation of a monument or a public place is its inscriptions. The words and symbols inscribed on a monument are meant to carry a direct message from its builder to posterity. To do so, they draw on a heritage that often stretches back in time. The Washington Monument has no inscription; its single symbolic reference is the obelisk itself. The pyramid on top perhaps recalls the pyramid on the great seal of the United States, the seal that is printed on the one dollar bill.

The shaft of an obelisk in ancient times was often covered with inscriptions and symbols detailing the great and mighty deeds of the hero it honored. For the Washington Monument, however, "severe simplicity" was preferred. Instead of reading the exterior faces of the shaft, visitors were invited to enter the monument through a door at its base, ascend the shaft by a stairway or by the construction elevator, and then look out at the city and the countryside spread before them. Here the new order for the ages was chiseled into the landscape. The monument, turned inside out, established a new type of inscription on the landscape itself.

It is not entirely accurate to say that no inscription was placed on Washington's needle. The apex of the pyramid is a piece of aluminum, about six pounds in weight (fig. 1-4). Three sides of this metal tip carry tiny inscriptions listing the names of the engineers and the commissioners, along with appropriate dates tracing the story of the monument's construction. The fourth side carries the Latin phrase "Laus Deo," or "praise to God." But nobody can see these inscriptions. We know about them only because they are recorded in the documents relating to the ceremony when the capstone was put in place.

Connections. The historian researching a monument's history will want to examine its connections with other people, places, and times. For the Washington Monument, connections to the heritage of Western civilization are easily discerned. The physical connections with all the states and territories are represented by the commemorative stones used in the interior. The monument also marked the national meridian, the line of longitude geographers used to start measuring the distance around the earth. The longitude of any place in the nineteenth century was usually given on American maps according to the degrees of distance from both the Greenwich and the Washington meridians.

The ways in which the monument represented duty, achievement, patriotism, and honor can be seen in its uses by American society. Figure 1-5 shows a certificate given to a schoolchild for punctual attendance in 1951, an award that boasted a color illustration of the Washington Monument. In 1934 a patent attorney soliciting clients described his firm in a booklet that featured a soaring view of the monument on its cover. The firm's serv-

ices were "as outstanding as the Washington Monument." Similar examples
could be gleaned from a variety of materials representing every decade and
every section of the nation.

Subsequent life. The more connections one can make between the actual
monument and other aspects of a community's life, the more one can document the success of the builders. The subsequent life of a monument thus

Fig. 1-4. Completing the Washington Monument. It was a very windy day when the capstone of the
Washington Monument was lowered into place on December 6, 1884. The stone is about three-feet
square at the base and about five feet in height. The scene shows the small aluminum cap being placed
on the very tip of the stone. "A moment afterwards the American flag was hoisted above the monument and cannon below were fired." From Stilson Hutchins and Joseph West Moore's, *The National
Capital: Past and Present* (1885).

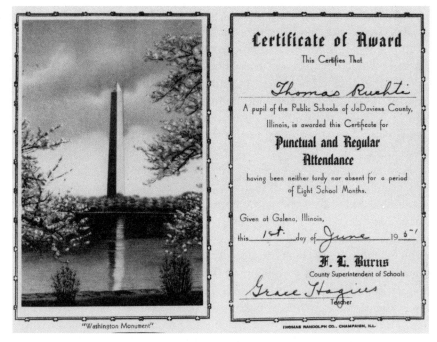

Fig. 1-5. Certificate of Award, 1951. This award for "punctual and regular attendance" was given to deserving students in JoDaviess County, Illinois, in the 1950s. The small certificate faces a full-color picture of the Washington Monument framed by the cherry trees in bloom. The whole piece was bound in a sturdy white folder with the flag and the salute printed on the cover.

provides some measure for evaluation. The Washington Monument, in its current simplified or "incomplete" state, could undoubtedly be changed or "finished" only with great difficulty. Any proposal to do so would provoke a great public outcry. Other monuments, however, can be moved or removed, remodeled or recast, modified or transformed, without protest. A statue interrupting the flow of traffic, for example, needs widespread community support to hold its ground against the arguments of traffic engineers and highway planners.

The subsequent life of a monument is often as instructive as its original purpose. In 1832, Congress decided to build a suitable memorial for George Washington by constructing a crypt for his tomb under the floor of the rotunda in the Capitol. This decision indirectly led to the formation of the private Washington Monument Society the following year. Congress meanwhile commissioned Horatio Greenough, a leading American sculptor, to fashion a statue to be placed above the tomb. The heirs of Washington, however, would not permit the general's bones to be moved from Mt. Vernon. Greenough, nevertheless, proceeded with his work, fashioned in the classical style to complement the architecture of the Capitol.

When the huge piece arrived from Italy in 1840, it could be placed in the rotunda only after the building's foundation was strengthened. The statue portrayed Washington half clad in a toga, seated on a Roman chair, with his right hand raised pointing to the sky (fig. 1-6). He looked like Zeus, a resemblance that Greenough thought appropriate, but the American public did not. The figure was soon moved out of the rotunda and placed on the Capitol grounds where a shed was built to cover it. After several more adaptations and moves, the statue eventually found a home in the Smithsonian Institution's Museum of American History. The monument had become an exhibit. Instead of occupying a place of honor beneath the dome of the Capitol, the twelve-ton statue was consigned to the "nation's attic."

Greenough's figure of an Olympian Washington is one of the few public monuments to be removed from the grounds of the complex of federal buildings in the capital city. Over the years, the place has been filled with monuments, turning L'Enfant's original design into a much more complicated city plan. Visitors to the Washington Monument today will note how the pantheon for American heroes originally proposed by Mills has materialized in a whole complex of memorials surrounding the obelisk.

Immediately to the west is the Lincoln Memorial, a Greek temple, designed by Henry Bacon, to house a very large figure of Abraham Lincoln by the celebrated sculptor Daniel Chester French. The story of this monument parallels the story of the Washington Monument. Congress organized a Lincoln Memorial Association in 1867, just two years after his death, but the idea languished. In 1911, new legislation finally led to the beginning of construction on land reclaimed from the Potomac River. Its dedication did not take place until after World War I. In contrast to the Washington Monument, the walls of Lincoln's Memorial are covered with inscriptions and paintings. His address at Gettysburg is inscribed in a place of honor on one wall, the speech itself being the most celebrated dedicatory oration in American history.

The Jefferson Memorial, to the south of the Washington Monument, is a Roman-style building also situated on a landfill area of the Potomac River. Since Abraham Lincoln was identified with the Republican Party and since he had been memorialized, many people felt that a president connected with the Democratic Party should also receive a suitable memorial. Franklin D. Roosevelt broke ground for the Jefferson Memorial in 1938, and the shrine was dedicated in the midst of World War II on the 200th birthday of the author of the Declaration of Independence, April 13, 1943. As in the Lincoln Memorial, a statue of the statesman and quotations from his writings are housed in the circular building.

Fig. 1-6. Greenough's Statue of Washington. Originally designed for interior use, the artist feared that its removal to the eastern grounds of the Capitol would disfigure the surface. An octagonal shed was therefore placed over it, but it proved to be distracting. By 1885, the date of this view, the shed had been removed. From Stilson Hutchins and Joseph West Moore's *The National Capital: Past and Present* (1885).

Not only have the styles of monuments changed over the years, but the purposes for which they are erected have changed as well. The Vietnam Veterans Memorial, set below the ground in the park lands that now occupy the landfill between the Washington Monument and the Lincoln Memorial, is an example of both kinds of changes. The visitor descends a winding stone pathway into the Constitution Gardens and confronts a V-shaped wall upon which are listed the names of all the military personnel who died in the conflict, inscribed in the order of their deaths. Visiting the wall, one veteran said, was "like walking into the war. You can feel us getting deeper and deeper into it, and more and more death." As one begins to leave the site, however, the shaft of the Washington Monument rises directly in front, a symbol of hope.

On the Vietnam Veterans Memorial, the inscriptions are overpowering; on the Washington Monument, inscriptions were thought unnecessary. In one monument, you must climb into the sky to see the symbolic inscription carved into the wilderness by the national experience. In the contemporary monument, you must descend into the earth itself. The documents of the Vietnam Veterans Memorial are now being stored in a Maryland warehouse. These are the items people have left at the base of the black granite wall. The first day the shrine was open to visitors, someone left a pair of cowboy boots beneath an inscribed name. Soon the offerings started coming in steady streams. Everyday something is left and is carefully added to the gifts in the memorial collection.

In his dedication oration a century before, Winthrop recalled a similar gift left by Benjamin Franklin for George Washington. In his will, the Philadelphia printer and statesman gave to "my friend and the friend of mankind" a walking stick with a gold head wrought in the shape of the cap of Liberty. "If it were a sceptre, he has merited it, and would become it."

Figure 1-7 summarizes the seven approaches for interpreting public places— approaches that are suggested by a brief consideration of the nation's attempt to erect a suitable monument to George Washington. The key source for the account was Winthrop's dedicatory oration, which was printed along with other speeches and relevant information as a government document. Similar books and pamphlets and comparable dedication addresses are available for a host of monuments in American history. To use them to best advantage, one might first want to consult some of the following guides to further study.

Public Monuments:
Seven Suggestions for Interpretation

1. History
2. Design
3. Materials
4. Site

5. Inscriptions
6. Connections
7. Subsequent life

Fig. 1-7.

Suggested Readings

To begin a study of monuments as public places, one should read the essays of John Brinckerhoff Jackson, the dean of American landscape historians, especially the title piece in his *The Necessity for Ruins and Other Topics* and "The Public Landscape." in *Landscapes*, both published in Amherst by the University of Massachusetts Press in 1980 and 1970, respectively. One should also note Daniel Boorstin's comments on "The American Style in Historical Monuments" in his *America and the Image of Europe* (New York: Meridian, 1960), pp. 81-96.

The story of the Washington Monument has been constructed from a variety of sources, the most helpful being *The Dedication of the Washington National Monument* (Washington, D.C.: Government Printing Office, 1885), which contains Robert C. Winthrop's oration, and the contemporary guidebook to *The National Capital: Past and Present* by Stilson Hutchins and Joseph West Moore (Washington, D.C.: The Post Publishing Company, 1885). One could trace the history of the Washington Monument by systematically exploring the guidebooks to the national capital. Lonnelle Aikman's illustrated essay on "The Monument: Tribute in Stone," a good history of the monument, was published as part of a pamphlet on *George Washington: Man and Monument* (Washington, D.C.: Washington National Monument Association, 1965). The most convenient source on Greenough's statue of Washington is Oliver W. Larkin's standard treatment of *Art and Life in America*, rev. ed. (New York: Holt, Rinehart and Winston, 1960), pp. 181-183.

The traveler's guides to American cities published in the nineteenth and early twentieth centuries are often excellent sources of information about public monuments, even those that no longer exist. The best of these volumes are found in the series produced and planned by Moses King of Boston between 1872 and the turn of the century. *King's Handbook of the United States* by M. F. Sweetser (available in many editions, such as the one published in Buffalo, New York, by Moses King Corporation in 1891) is worth consulting. This printing has more than 2,600 illustrations—a treasure house for drawing comparisons between cities. More than a dozen monuments honoring Washington, for example, are illustrated.

In 1825, Daniel Webster delivered the most celebrated American oration connected with public monuments. His conclusion at the laying of the cornerstone of the Bunker Hill

Monument summarizes the purpose of the structure: "There remains to us a great duty of defense and preservation. . . Let our age be the age of improvement. . . And, by the blessing of God, may that country itself become a vast and splendid monument, not of oppression and terror, but of wisdom, of peace, and of liberty, upon which the world may gaze with admiration forever!" Webster gave another notable speech at the dedication of the monument in 1843, a speech which undoubtedly was used by Winthrop in writing his 1885 oration.

The most creative interpretation of the Bunker Hill monument is Daniel J. Boorstin's connection between the construction of the monument and the origins of the New England granite industry: *The Americans: The National Experience* (New York: Random House, 1965), pp. 17-19. Boorstin points out how the problem of transporting the granite blocks for the monument led to one of the first railroads in the United States. To ship the blocks, Gridley Bryant developed some fundamental devices used in the subsequent development of the railroad: the eight-wheel car, the switch, the turntable, and so on. The builders themselves heeded Webster's call for an age of improvement!

·2·

Buildings

THE WASHINGTON MONUMENT WAS MEANT TO STAND alone, but most buildings, whether public or private, are part of a group, or an ensemble, which is often called the "cityscape." The documentation for individual buildings—blueprints, photographs, and promotional brochures—it is true, often presents the structures in isolation, removed from their contexts. But when one experiences buildings in reality, they are always embedded in an environment, whether of landscape or cityscape.

When a building is placed in the context of the built environment, it acquires, by definition, a public aspect. Thus all structures in a community, whether village, town, or city, have public dimensions. By facing a public path or road, they become part of the streetscape. In almost every case, the street, as a public thoroughfare, was there before the building. Each structure subsequently took its place along the avenue according to the space assigned to it by the public, or political, decision about how to shape the environment. The fundamental plan of a community was set by dividing the area into public streets or spaces and individual lots or tracts. Thus the decisions that shape the character of any particular building are really a mixture of prior political choices and later individual considerations.

John Brinckerhoff Jackson, in an essay on "The Public Landscape," has suggested that we use the concept of a large building, the megastructure, in our thinking about a community as a whole. The large building, or the public landscape, provides all the necessary facilities for individuals to come and go or to arrange individual offices or apartments according to their needs and interests. The skyscraper is like a city unto itself, and conversely, the city is like a skyscraper. A consideration of the relationship between buildings and the city, the intertwining of public and private spaces, is a good place to continue our examination of the nature of public places.

17

With the advent of inexpensive paper and mechanized printing in the nineteenth century, developers, local boosters, and real estate firms produced promotional brochures on most of the important buildings in American cities. Sometimes these small publications took the form of travel guides; in other cases, they advertised individual buildings or developments. In all cases, however, the mood was upbeat, and the purpose was to sell or to impress. These promotional brochures are of great use to historians constructing the history of a building.

The promotional brochures fall naturally into two groups: those devoted to an individual building and those concerned with a whole area or city. This chapter will explore how these brochures serve as sources for the study of the history of public buildings. For a variety's sake, let us jump a generation from Robert Winthrop's dedicatory oration to about the year 1914 and consider two buildings whose stories are similar to that of the Washington Monument. The first is actually a group of municipal buildings in Springfield, Massachusetts. The second is a skyscraper in New York City.

The Springfield Civic Center

Progressive Springfield, Massachusetts was published by George S. Graves in that city in 1914. He described the unpaged pamphlet as a "conducted tour of sixty Phototype views showing the leading features that make this City of Homes attractive for business, residence and pleasure." The brochure is crammed with pictures, illustrations, and text. Although a price of ten cents is printed on the title page of the first edition, the second edition is stamped "Compliments of the Springfield National Bank."

The cover of the pamphlet features an architectural drawing of the new Civic Center of Springfield (fig. 2-1). The drawing wraps around the piece, so that the Campanile and the Municipal Building dominate the front cover while the Auditorium extends to the back cover. Since the Civic Center was dedicated on December 8, 1913, it was appropriate that ten of the thirty pages in the 1914 booklet should be devoted to the new complex. The edifice marked "a new era in the progress of the city" and "made Springfield the most talked about city in America."

Our consideration starts with a page that features three striking photographs of the building: in daylight, at dusk, and "illuminated with 3000 electric lights" on the first night of the dedication proceedings. Flanking the first picture are two comparable views, one from the Old World and one from the New; the Campanile in Venice and the Washington Monument. The text of the booklet asks: "Why go to Venice? Why go to Washington?" The observation deck, the pamphlet continues, "will be a Mecca to which people will journey from afar to behold the glories of Springfield and the Connecticut Valley." The next several pages then present various photographs taken from the top of the Campanile.

The impression one gets from these views, along with other aerial perspectives included in Graves's publication, is how closely the various buildings and structures of the city are related to each other and tied to the basic plan of the city. After these four pages, however, the rest of the booklet concentrates on presenting individual buildings and structures as set pieces, largely removed from their urban contexts.

In most views, it is true, a street appears in the foreground with a variety of reminders that we are looking at the public facade of the building. The scene in front of the United States Post Office and Custom House is crowded

Fig. 2-1. *Progressive Springfield, Massachusetts.* The formal appearance of the Civic Center, its symmetry and classical proportions, made it a source of public and civic aspiration. The formalism was an appropriate public statement for a grand entry into the city. A community that built "America's finest civic group" of buildings must have great promise in the future. The promotional brochure, however, probably went a bit too far in claiming that "in all the world there is nothing like these architectural gems." The illustration forms the wrap-around cover for the second edition of the promotional brochure issued by George S. Graves in 1914.

MAIN STREET, SPRINGFIELD, MASSACHUSETTS
From Hotel Worthy and Post Office to Court Square and Masonic Building at State Street.

Fig. 2-2. Main Street, Springfield, Massachusetts. Although all eyes seem to be focused on the parade in this photograph, the modern observer is struck by how well the commercial buildings relate to the pedestrians. The taller structures are composed of a series of two- or three-story elevations, each with a little cornice. A large, ornate cornice at the top relates the building to the street. Pedestrians had a lot of decorative elements to observe and a variety of architectural styles to enjoy. From George S. Graves's *Progressive Springfield, Massachusetts* (1914).

with pedestrians, and the street sign close to the camera clearly reads "Main Street." On another page, the only way for the photographer to include both buildings that constituted the Hotel Worth in one picture was to include similar structures across the street and down the block. But the best view of the buildings situated in their context is the photograph of Main Street (fig. 2-2). The viewer is immediately impressed by the crowds jamming the sidewalks and spilling onto the street. The caption notes that 300,000 people trade in Springfield. "Rain or shine. . . a million dollars is an ordinary day's business here." A close inspection of the photograph reveals that it was taken on the day of a parade. A marching band is just leaving the picture, and the four automobiles are apparently carrying dignitaries. It was not an everyday scene.

The buildings lining Main Street provide an impressive backdrop for this civic occasion, each one joining the others to create an ornamental facade. Every structure has its own architectural design and its own personality, yet each seems to take its assigned place in the city plan, varying hardly an inch in approaching the sidewalk. The assorted ornaments and cornices blend together in a harmonious whole, and the flags provide a sort of punctuation tying the whole scene together and reminding everyone of the public nature of the whole place.

The focus of public life in Springfield was Court Square. This open space extending to the Connecticut River was laid out as a formal park in 1819. As the historical core of the city, the square had become, by 1914 "the central breathing spot" of Springfield. Churches, theaters, and commercial buildings lined two sides of the square, while the new civic buildings faced the river. Here was Springfield's harbor as well as its "front door." A visitor arriving by boat would enter the city through Court Square. The formal Renaissance architecture of the Civic Center thus became the focal point of the cityscape. At the core, dominating the scene, stood the 300-foot tower. The buildings with templed facades on either side gave the Campanile a solid base from which to rise. Unlike the Washington Monument, the Springfield tower was designed to fit into a complex of buildings. It served as the visual focal point at the very heart of the city.

The pamphlet, in various places, refers to the many ways in which the Campanile served as a public building. It marked the location of the Civic Center "above the trees." The clock on its face told the time of day, while its bells sounded out each quarter hour during the day and each hour at night. After dark, the lighted tower was a beacon, "its brilliantly lighted

apex reminding all beholders that Springfield is on the map." Two poems
in the pamphlet refer to "the guardian tower," and another uses the phrase,
"mighty landmark in a mighty land." Elevators took visitors to the balco-
nies above the clock, from which "picturesque Springfield and the incom-
parable Connecticut Valley" could be seen at its best.

The most suggestive page in the brochure is the one devoted to the tower's
bells, which provided "the city's voice." The text reveals, in a unique way,
the interrelationship between public and private elements that exist in almost
all buildings. The Campanile housed a set of twelve bells, but only the largest
one was purchased with public funds. Individuals and groups, including the
children of the public schools and the members of the Board of Trade, donated
the rest. Thus the sounds of the city represented, like its buildings and its
cityscape, a blend of public and private decision making. The large bell tolled
out the hours, day and night, while some of the bells given as gifts divided
the daylight hours into quarters. The "general chimes" used the full complement of bells, both public and private in origin, to give voice to the city.

The Woolworth Tower

During 1913, the year in which the public first heard the peal of the Springfield bells, the Woolworth Tower in New York City was completed. Its promotional brochure, *Above the Clouds and Old New York* by H. Addington Bruce
(1913), addressed visitors to the new skyscraper. The same type of publication as the Springfield booklet, *Above the Clouds and Old New York* is larger
and more ornate in appearance. An embossed cover uses gold ink; full-color
photographs appear in the book; and special line drawings illustrate the text.

The tower in New York, of course, was a much larger and more expensive
structure than Springfield's Campanile. From 1913 until 1930, the Woolworth Tower was the world's tallest building. Since the brochure was issued
by the company, it focused on the firm's corporate headquarters rather than
on the city as a whole.

In some ways, Bruce must have thought it was desirable to isolate the skyscraper from its urban context, hence the emphasis on being "above the
clouds" (fig. 2-3), transcending the earthbound city and forming, as it were,
a whole community by itself. "In this gigantic pile it is estimated that 7,000
to 10,000 tenants will be housed—a number large enough to form a small
municipality, with a mayor, executive departments and police force," the text
explains. The skyline of New York, Bruce notes, was like "serried peaks"

THE WOOLWORTH BUILDING IS EQUIPPED WITH 26 OTIS ELEVATORS. TWO
OF THEM RUN FROM THE FIRST TO THE FIFTY-FIRST FLOOR—680 FEET. THE
GREATEST DISTANCE SERVED BY ANY SINGLE PASSENGER ELEVATOR. A
SHUTTLE ELEVATOR CARRIES THE VISITORS FROM THE FIFTY-FIRST TO
THE FIFTY-FOURTH FLOOR, THE OBSERVATION STATION

Fig. 2-3. *Above the Clouds*: The Woolworth Building, 1913. This illustration from the pamphlet by
H. Addington Bruce emphasizes the vertical system of transportation within the skyscraper. Much
of the talk about these massive structures centered on how they were, in effect, cities within themselves. Thus the discussion of the elevators often used a vocabulary of the mass transportation system:
cars, express routes, shuttle elevators, and upright tracks. One of the great marvels of the age was
that one could ascend above the clouds without climbing a single stair. From H. Addington Bruce's
Above the Clouds and Old New York (1913).

made by the commercial buildings, towers, and church steeples, all contending
with one another for a position of privilege. "But above them all rises the
Woolworth building, calm and unassailable."

Thus in one sense the tower was detached from the city, yet the reader
is struck by the number of illustrations in the booklet that relate the structure to its urban context. While the cover shows the peak of the tower iso-
lated above the clouds, the frontispiece relates the building to its immediate
surroundings and even extends the perspective far enough to include the
rival Singer Building in the view. The last page of the booklet is a full color
view of "the ever changing sky-line of New York." The Woolworth Tower
is definitely the highest point in the cityscape, but other tall buildings are
given places of honor, especially the Singer Building and the Metropolitan
Life Tower.

Some statistics for each of these superstar structures are even listed in the
Woolworth booklet: "A comparison of the three great towers of New York
is interesting as showing the remarkable progress made year by year in the
development of the skyscraper." The conclusion seemed to be that, given
a few years, even the Woolworth Tower would be left behind in the sweep
of progress.

A sense of time and its inevitable limitations thus crept into Bruce's story.
But a recognition of the passing years had been on the author's mind from
the very beginning. (Note that the title of the promotional pamphlet is *Above
the Clouds and Old New York*.) The publication is really two booklets in
one: a celebration of the skyscraper and a history of old New York. Most
of the text and the line drawings are devoted to the history of the site, while
the photographs celebrate the triumph of the new building. "Almost from
the beginnings of New York, the ground on which the wonderful Woolworth Building stands . . . has been directly or indirectly associated with
important events in the history of the city."

A visitor to the new building, or perhaps people who were about to take
up their jobs in its offices, needed to digest almost a dozen pages of historical narrative to appreciate the place. History provided as much of a context
for the building as viewing it as part of the cityscape. The new skyscraper
rose from a plot of land that was once part of the provision farm for the
Dutch West India Company. Here the city's first skyscraper, "the old windmill," was erected in 1631 (fig. 2-4).

Later a large mansion was built on the site, and in 1822, it became the

Fig. 2-4. "The First Skyscraper." The connection of skyscapers like the Woolworth Building with history and tradition was most obviously expressed by the use of architectural styles and motifs gathered from the past. But the author of the building's first promotional brochure also devoted most of the pamphlet's text to making explicit connections between the site of the building and history of the metropolis. "To an extent unsuspected by any except the historian, it has had a really noteworthy place in New York's evolution." From H. Addington Bruce's *Above the Clouds and Old New York* (1913).

residence of Philip Hone. He became mayor of New York in 1826 after acquiring a fortune in commerce. As a leader of New York society, he devoted his life to public affairs and the promotion of culture. His house became a gathering place for artists and writers. In 1836, the expanding commerce of the city pushed Hone and his circle to a new location, and the old mansion was converted into a place of business.

When Frank W. Woolworth decided to build an office complex on the site, he realized the potential a great building had to advertise his five-and-ten cent stores. To help achieve this goal, Woolworth did not turn to the architect of one of the leading skyscrapers of the day; instead he selected Cass Gilbert, a prominent designer of public buildings. Gilbert had just completed the magnificent Minnesota State Capitol in 1905 and the Customhouse in New York City in 1907, both structures regarded as masterpieces. Later he would design the United States Supreme Court building. As the plans for Woolworth's building evolved, the concept became larger and larger.

Additional property was added to the site, and the final proposal called for erecting a structure nearly a hundred feet higher than its tallest rival in the United States (but still nearly 200 feet shorter than the Eiffel Tower in Paris).

The architectural style of the edifice was just as important as its great size. Indeed, the building's design was as much of a challenge as an opportunity. The Singer Building (fig. 2-5), erected in 1908, was the first structure in the United States to reach 600 feet in height. It eclipsed the Washington Monument but, at the same time, posed the problem of how a skyscraper should look. Its architect used a French Second Empire style to give the tall structure some grace, but the effort was not thought to be entirely successful. The design of the Metropolitan Life Building (fig. 2-6), which followed in 1909, used the Campanile on St. Mark's Square in Venice for its model, a design followed in a more literal fashion by the architect of the Springfield Civic Center.

Not only was the Woolworth Tower planned to be nearly a hundred feet higher than the Metropolitan Life Tower, but its design also called for the skyscraper to rise from a large block-like building at the base. Gilbert thought Gothic ornamentation would be best for the structure; the vertical emphasis of that style seemed appropriate for a towering building, and the delicate details of flying buttresses, gargoyles, and Gothic sculpture would give a light and airy feeling to a building reaching "above the clouds." The decorations for the tower also provided the opportunity for a bit of whimsy in the medieval manner. In one place, the architect is pictured holding a model of the building; in another, Woolworth, himself, is featured counting his nickles and dimes.

When completed in 1913, the Woolworth Tower was an immediate hit with the public. President Woodrow Wilson threw a switch at the White House, and the building lit up. The Reverend S. Parker Cadman called is "a cathedral of commerce," and company officials immediately liked the name. In 1917, when a new promotional booklet replaced the original *Above the Clouds and Old New York*, it was titled *The Cathedral of Commerce*, and Cadman contributed the foreword.

Cass Gilbert set down his ideal for public buildings: they should set before the people, in a concrete example, the "imponderable elements of life and character." Cadman acknowledged the success Gilbert had achieved along these lines in the Woolworth Tower. It was, he said, hailed as the city's foremost building "by those who aspire to perfection, and by those who use visible things to obtain it."

Singer Building, and Part of Financial District, New York City.

Fig. 2-5. The Singer Building. The Singer Building, completed in 1908, was the first structure in America to surpass the Washington Monument in height. For a time, it stood about 200 feet above its nearest rival. By the time this post card view was made, it had been joined and surpassed by several other soaring buildings. Although it was the first great twentieth-century skyscraper in New York, the Singer Building was not used as a prototype. The fact that the structure was wider at the top stories seemed to limit its soaring qualities. Perhaps it followed too closely the tradition of Main Street architecture, like the styles noted in fig. 2-2.

Fig. 2-6. Metropolitan Life Building. The 700-foot Metropolitan Life Building replaced the Singer Building as "the highest building in the world" in 1909. It held that position until the completion of the Woolworth Building four years later. Like the Campanile in the Springfield Civic Center, the tower was directly inspired by the Campanile of St. Mark's Square in Venice. To complete the parallel, the New York edifice had a series of bells. The bells dictated a clock, but, given the height of the structure, the clock had to be of an immense size to be read from the street. The diameter of the clock face was more than 26 feet. This post card view was published by Valentine and Son's Publishing Company, New York.

The promotional spirit thus animated these brochures on individual buildings and their cities. But the information and the illustrations they contain make them valuable sources for historians. The brochures, of course, must be used with care and placed into the context of other documentation. But they should also be used with an alertness to the interpretive suggestions they contain. They recite, as a constant refrain, the dynamic between the public and private aspects of any building.

In our discussion, we have noted how the Civic Center in Springfield served as the visual focal point for the community, documenting its cultural roots in the traditions of Western civilization, and announcing the city's aspirations for the future. Even these civic buildings depended, in part, on the support of individuals and private groups. The Woolworth Tower, although privately owned, played a similar role and addressed the public with a similar message. Its promoters even insisted that its context extend beyond the contemporary cityscape to the historical associations of the site itself.

Interpreting Buildings

In considering the two promotional brochures and the two buildings, a variety of interpretive paths have been sighted. First, the list of seven approaches, developed in chapter 1 for monuments, can be applied to buildings. Then the following list of considerations will help the historian pose some fundamental questions when developing a research plan for the history of any building, emphasizing its public character.

History. Obelisks, campaniles, and skyscrapers have a lot in common if the examples we have considered are characteristic. Not only does each have a history of its own, but also each reaches back in time to specific precedents. Thus it is helpful to know something about Renaissance architecture in studying the Springfield Civic Center and at least a basic knowledge of Gothic construction when examining the Woolworth Tower.

Under the history rubric, one might set up a basic chronology for the individual story of each structure. Various important events could be recorded on a time line, and the list divided into appropriate stages in the story of a building: planning, construction, and set-up or dedication.

Design. The more the creators of a building take its public character seriously, the more importance they usually attach to design and ornamentation. Each of the structures discussed so far was designed by a professional architect who reached back to the Old World for an appropriate model. There seems to be a clear message here: If one wants to understand American buildings, especially those of public nature, one needs some knowledge of Western civilization.

Materials. The public buildings in Springfield were dressed in Indiana limestone. The Woolworth Tower was completely covered with glazed terra cotta. Literally "baked earth," terra cotta as a building material became popular in the early twentieth century. Clay was placed in molds, baked, and glazed to provide a relatively inexpensive ornamental covering for buildings. The material was fireproof, easy to install, and could be kept sparkling clean with little effort. Terra cotta was also used in the interior of many buildings. As Bruce's pamphlet on the Woolworth Tower explained, "the building is absolutely fireproof; there was no wood used in its construction, the doors, partitions, and trim being of steel, terra cotta and wire glass."

Site. The importance of the site for the Springfield Civic Center was emphasized in a variety of ways in the pamphlet, although a map of the center of the city was not included. *Above the Clouds* has a map showing the site of the Woolworth Tower, but it is dated 1723, nearly two centuries before the time of the building . The point of Bruce's text, of course, was to emphasize the historical associations of the site and not to provide an up-to-date map of the area. Just as a researcher would construct a basic chronology to use in studying a building, so he or she would also want to have a large-scale map available showing the specific site of the structure and its surroundings.

Inscriptions and iconography. Both the Springfield Civic Center and the Woolworth Tower carried a whole collection of inscriptions and iconographic decorations, but these were largely ignored by the promotional pamphlets, both in the text and in their illustrations. In the single exception, the editor carefully included in the brochure the texts of several lengthy inscriptions on the bells of Springfield's Campanile. Nevertheless, both pamphlets preferred to look at the structure as a whole, to take the entire complex as a symbolic statement, rather than to concentrate on its details.

Connections. The Springfield pamphlet implicitly connected the Civic Center to the rest of the city in a spatial sense. Bruce, on the other hand, was quite explicit in connecting the Woolworth Tower to the history of the city. He concluded his account by emphasizing another important connection: how the building was tied to the metropolitan area by the network of public transportation. His concluding paragraph noted that "176 miles of new subways and elevated lines" were planned in 1913. When these were complete, "within three or four years, passengers from Brooklyn, from all parts of Manhattan, the Bronx, Queens, and Richmond will be landed either at the door or within a block of the Woolworth Building." When studying public places in large cities, the historian needs contemporaneous maps of public transportation routes. A functioning public transportation system was, after all, a prerequisite to any skyscraper construction.

Subsequent life. Neither promotional brochure spelled out any expectations for the subsequent life of the buildings. By nature, both publications looked to an optimistic future. The Woolworth pamphlet, to be sure, emphasized the changes that came with the passage of time and nowhere suggested that the tower would be immune from these forces. It is interesting to note, however, that the *Illustrated Guide to the Treasures of America*, published by the Reader's Digest Association in 1974, still listed the Springfield buildings and the Woolworth Tower "as fascinating places to visit." The skyscraper received one of the 5,000 individual entries in the book and a descriptive paragraph. The municipal group in Springfield was noted in an appendix, "More Treasures to Enjoy," with a comment about the "panoramic view from the 300-foot observation tower." The Campanile and the skyscraper thus still functioned a half century later according to the original plans of their builders.

Figure 2-7 provides a series of questions to ask when considering various ways to come to terms with the history of a building. The checklist speaks for itself, but the reader should also note the commentary on individual types of buildings given in chapter 6.

Questions to Consider When Studying a Building

I. Basic Questions
  A. Who built this building?
  B. Why was it built?
  C. When was it planned, and when was it completed?
  D. Who were its architect and its developer?

II. Some Public Aspects
  A. How does the building relate to the street and to its immediate surroundings?
  B. What elements make the structure part of a group?
  C. Is this a monumental building or a landmark? If so, what characteristics give it this quality?
  D. How do pedestrians and passers-by relate to the building?
  E. How is the building connected to the community as a whole?

III. Some Private Aspects
  A. What makes this building unique?
  B. How has the building been used and adapted over the years?
  C. How was the building financed? Who paid for its construction and maintenance?
  D. What is the architectural style of the building and its decorations?
  E. Does the building say anything about a particular person or group?

IV. The People Dimension
  A. Does this building say anything about the people who built it or used it?
  B. How does the structure manage people or influence their attitudes and behavior?
  C. Are concepts of class, status, race, or ethnicity useful in interpreting the building? If so, in what ways?
  D. Does the structure tend to isolate people or bring them together?
  E. How does the building recognize that it is part of a community?

V. Site and Situation
  A. How does the building fit into the community's plan?
  B. Has the physical geography of the site influenced the structure?
  C. What is the relationship between the site and the transportation patterns of the community?
  D. How is the building situated on its lot?
  E. Do zoning laws or landmark regulations affect the building or its site?

VI. The Time Dimension
   A. How has this site been used by people in the past?
   B. How has the community around the building changed over time? Has the site or the structure reflected these changes?
   C. To what extent was the building designed to reflect historical styles, and to what extent was it innovative in character?
   D. Has the structure been remodeled or adapted to meet changing conditions?
   E. How can the history of the building or the site be divided into periods?

Fig. 2-7.

Suggested Readings

Promotional brochures, such as the two discussed in this chapter, have often survived only by luck. Most of the time, they were discarded when they became "out of date." If they were ever saved in the first place, they were most commonly placed in the vertical files of libraries and ephemera boxes in historical societies. Scrapbooks and architectural collections, too, are good places to look for these types of brochures.

Similar information is often recorded, but with much briefer treatment, in the American Guide Series, first prepared under the Federal Writers' Project of the Works Progress Administration in the 1930s. Many of these guides have been reprinted or revised and updated. The original plan was to have a volume for every state. Several cities, counties, and towns also had separate publications. The materials used to compile the guides in the 1930s were sometimes placed in public depositories.

For the histories of individual buildings, contact local groups interested in historical preservation. The local chapter of the American Institute of Architects can usually locate individuals who have done research on buildings in a particular area. The Society of Architectural Historians has a number of active local groups and also publishes a quarterly journal. People who collect post cards are often the best sources of information on where to locate pamphlets issued for visitors to towns and buildings. Frequently, the janitor, engineer, or the manager of a building can locate helpful sources of information. A maintenance worker in a celebrated Chicago skyscraper once pulled an early promotional brochure from between two large pipes when a student told him what he was trying to locate.

If you are interested in the changing styles of public buildings and the forces that shaped them, page through *The Federal Presence: Architecture, Politics, and National Design* by Lois Craig and the staff of the Federal Architecture Project (Cambridge, Mass.: MIT Press, 1977, re-issued in a paperback edition in 1984). This book's extensive bibliography, with its emphasis on periodical articles, is still a gold mine for suggestions, although it includes publications only up to 1976.

There are many books on the history of American architecture in general and on the skyscraper in particular. *The Architecture of America: A Social and Cultural History* by John Burchard and Albert Bush-Brown (Boston: Little, Brown, 1966) is always worth consulting. For beginning students, the two-volume paperback *American Architecture* by Marcus Whiffen and Frederick Koeper, (Cambridge, Mass.: MIT Press, 1983) is a good, clear discussion. *Identifying American Architecture: A Pictorial Guide to Styles and Terms, 1600-1945* by John J.-G. Blumenson (Nashville: American Association for State and Local History, 1977) is a handy companion when looking at a building from the perspective of an art historian.

The best source on the Woolworth Tower is Paul Goldberger, *The Skyscraper* (New York: Alfred A. Knopf, 1981), which features the tower "above the clouds" on its title page. Chapter 1 discusses the Singer Building and its predecessors in New York. Chapter 3 features the Woolworth Tower. Anyone interested in the comments by critics of the time should consult Montgomery Schuyler's "The Towers of Manhattan," *Architectural Record* (February, 1913). The re-creation of past cityscapes in New York after the fashion of H. Addington Bruce's pamphlet has been done in drawings and a brief text by J. Ernest Brierly in *The Streets of Old New York* (New York: Hastings House, 1953). John A. Kouwenhoven's *The Columbia Historical Portrait of New York* (New York: Harper and Row, 1972) is a masterpiece and worth consulting by people interested in any American city.

This chapter has emphasized that all buildings have a public dimension and must be considered as part of the total context of the built environment. This approach can best be pursued by reading the brief history of the *American Skyline* by Christopher Tunnard and Henry Hope Reed (Boston: Houghton Mifflin, 1955). The idea of using promotional brochures as a way to begin the study of buildings was suggested by Anselm L. Strauss in his seminal book, *Images of the American City* (New Brunswick, N.J.: Transaction Books, 1976). Chapter 1, "The City as a Whole," and chapter 5, "The Visitor's View: The City Appreciated," are good places to start any study of the urban fabric.

·3·

Town Plans

THE VIEW FROM ON TOP, WHETHER FROM THE WASHINGTON Monument, the Springfield Campanile, or the Woolworth Tower, provides a splendid perspective on the city as a whole. Before a visitor starts sorting out the patterns below, before he or she begins searching for details, the community appears as a single artifact. It is the creation of the people as a whole, the architectural manifestation of the corporate charter, the civic container, the megastructure in which the individual lives of citizens go their various ways.

The view, itself, can be an object lesson in geography, an aesthetic experience, or an emotional encounter. But it also can provide a civic education, for visitors can see the totality of the built environment as the end result of people joining together in a government. They can catch the manifestation of the community as a corporate force. The image of the city set on a hill, viewed from a distant perspective, has had a powerful influence on the American imagination, but in the center of town, the soaring edifice, which enables people to look down on the city and see it as a whole, is of no less importance.

Even today, an aerial perspective highlights the public nature of places. Stand in the visitor's shoes on an observation platform and note the sequence of analysis: First, the impression of the whole; second, the recognition of geography, the division of the scene into land and water, and a feel for the impact of topography and the physical landscape; third, the shaping of the city into a plan according to the pattern of its streets and the division of its spaces; finally, the search for landmarks and familiar places and, when one has located a place, relating it, in reverse order, to the contexts first perceived, of city plan, of geography, and then of losing it in the mystery of the whole vision.

The focus in this chapter is on stage three, the plan of a community as a whole as well as the public ways and streets that define and set that plan. To explore this type of public place, we turn for our sources to city plans, town maps, plats, and a variety of cartographic materials.

The Nebraska Sunday-School Assembly

In the first two chapters, we have focused on prominent structures along the eastern coast of the nation. This chapter moves the location to the American interior and finds an example less famous, a community that is no more.

The map pictured in figure 3-1 was found in a large box of papers cleaned out of an attic and carted to a flea market. It was a stationery map of the type not uncommon in the late nineteenth century. Maps of railroad routes, real estate developments, and town subdivisions often were printed on the back of business letters as an early form of advertising by mail.

The document provides an opportunity to study the plan of a community now almost forgotten. There are many details on the map, and careful historians have a way of exploring as many of them as possible, gleaning suggestions for interpretation as well as bits of information. The Nebraska Sunday-School Assembly near Crete, Nebraska, by legal definition was a private corporation, and in the strict sense, not a public place. But, as we have seen, the sharp division of places into public and private spheres often misses the community context that binds both types of real estate into a whole. If we first look at community building in the private sphere, where the story is usually less complex, the basic themes will stand out more clearly. Moreover, almost every American town and city had its origins, at least in part, in this type of private initiative.

How should we begin to study this Nebraska community? The first thing we need is another map. This is always the case when using large-scale maps. (The scale of a map refers to the ratio between the distance on the map and the equivalent distance on the ground.) On our map, an inch equals about 350 feet. Thus Big Blue River, about 100 feet wide, appears as a thick quarter-inch ribbon winding its way across the paper. The stationery's size dictated that, with this large scale, only about a mile of the river's course could be included.

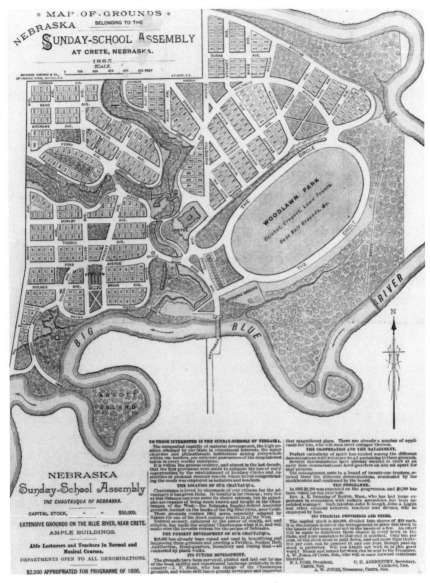

Fig. 3-1. Map of Grounds belonging to the Nebraska Sunday-School Assembly at Crete, Nebraska (1885). The map is on the back of stationery with the printed heading of Abbott & Abbott, Lawyers, Crete, Nebraska. Many of these stationery maps appeared in the late nineteenth century as advertising pieces, especially for real estate developments and railroads. The map was produced in Buffalo, New York, not far from the original Chautauqua institution.

The "Official Highway Map of Nebraska," to which we turn to locate the town of Crete, uses a much smaller scale. On the highway map, an inch represents almost twenty miles. By using the index, it is possible to find Crete in a few seconds, near the intersection of "L-26" on the map's location grid. Situated in the southeastern part of the state, Crete is only one inch, or about twenty miles, from Lincoln, the state capital. The river now shows up as a faint blue line flowing southward in a fairly straight course because the small scale of the highway map does not permit the recording of meandering details. The larger the scale of the map, the general rule goes, the more detailed is its portrayal.

Now that the highway map has given us a sense of where the Nebraska Sunday-School Assembly was located, let us consider the general plan of the grounds. The river, the most conspicuous feature on the map, provides at times a boundary for the property but also subtly structures the overall plan of the community. In this respect, the river seems to be in a state of tension with the rectilinear plan of land division, which has set most of the other boundaries according to the cardinal directions. The directional symbol pointing north in the right-hand corner of the map helps one develop this hypothesis. A single measurement confirms it.

The township and range system of land division was used for the survey and sale of most public lands located beyond the boundaries of the original states. First proposed in the Land Ordinance of 1785 and then confirmed by Congress under the Constitution, the townships, six miles square and divided into thirty-six sections, structured the landscape across the continent. The basic unit of land division soon became forty acres, or one-sixteenth of a square-mile section. Since a forty-acre square measures 1,320 feet on each side, a researcher will often look for this dimension on a map. On the large-scale map, it is exactly the distance from the eastern boundary of the tract to the center of the entrance road or its continuance as Abernethy Avenue, the north-south axis of the community plan. It is also the measurement from the northern-most point of the grounds to the hotel area at the center and from the western-most part of the development to the center of the north-south axis. We might conclude, therefore, that the Assembly Grounds were created out of a quarter section of land, or four forty-acre plots. The hotel was apparently located near the center of the quarter section, and Abernethy and Bowlby avenues divided the quarter section into four quadrants.

The street pattern, in places, follows the grid-iron model dictated by the township system. In other areas, the basic topography seems to dictate a series of curving avenues. These outline the small creek, which enters the Big Blue River just west of the entrance to the grounds and then divides into two branches near the hotel. A third category of streets includes those placed on a diagonal, set on an oval, or curved according to the artistic taste of the person who laid out the plat.

The original map employed colors to indicate the various land uses within the community. The river is blue, and the wooded areas and parks are green by convention. The individual lots are pink, and the major public buildings and structures are orange.

The low-lying areas along the river and the creek have been left in a natural state for passive recreation. Woodlawn Park and several other places have been cleared and arranged for public uses. Thus the map indicates that the park area within The Circle would be used for "cricket, croquet, lawn tennis, base ball grounds, &c." The fact that this is a low-lying area can be seen by the steep bank indicated by hatchures along Doane Avenue. The hotel is thus situated on something like a promontory. A close inspection of the map reveals that the flooding of the river was controlled by a dam and a levee along the eastern margin of the tract. The boathouse at the northern end of the levee takes advantage of the regulated water above the dam.

This boathouse, colored orange on the map, is one of the public buildings. The hotel occupies the most prominent place of all the public buildings. Near it, across the creek, is the Normal Hall for formal classes. The text at the bottom of the map refers to the Sunday-School Assembly as "the Chautauqua of Nebraska," imitating the popular Western New York institution, which combined a vacation retreat with the formal education of Sunday School teachers and provided recreation and cultural up-lift for middle-class families. "Its locality is far from us; very few at this distance can ever enter its choice retreats, but its principles are capable of being made known and taught [here] at the Chautauqua of the West." Instruction for teachers at Normal Hall was supplemented by lectures, concerts, and public programs at the Pavilion in the southwest portion of the grounds.

The individual lots, all numbered, were available for sale, and the promoters expected that cottages would soon be erected on them. The "public" buildings were owned, in this case, by the stockholders in the assembly. Five thousand shares of capital stock, with a face value of $10 each, were to be sold "in every town in the State," at 10 percent down and with at least three years to pay the balance. The "public" buildings were all in place, and $1,200 had been spent on various programs during 1885, the initial year of the project. More than double that amount had been allotted for the 1886 season.

The community plan had thus been established by a corporation, which had secured financial backing and purchased a tract of land. It then hired J. F. Hunt, a landscape architect, who developed the community plan by laying out the streets, providing for public areas, and dividing some of the land into private lots. Additional funds were spent on public improvements such as the dam, the levee, the park, and a variety of bridges scattered throughout the grounds. Buildings for the Chautauqua were then built along with a hotel to house and feed its participants. Private enterprise had paralleled the process of public town building in creating this educational and recreational facility.

Close inspection of the plan also suggests that the original planners carefully arranged the community so that certain functions were segregated from others. The planners made the entrance to the community more formal by offsetting the entry bridge to the east of the access road. Thus one approached the bridge from a small square. Also note how, after crossing the river, the visitor found a "hitching ground" at the foot of the bridge to segregate the horses from the residential areas. Next the visitor faced a pair of curving streets, no doubt with a formal flower garden between them.

The individual lots to the right were meant for commercial rather than residential use. This "Market Place" was the shopping center for the community. East of the formal entryway was the large park; to the north was the hotel complex; and to the west, in the middle of Foss Avenue, was the office or administration building. Continuing west on Foss Avenue, the visitor would reach the large Pavilion, and beyond that, by taking the curving Gough Avenue, the visitor could cross a foot bridge to a sylvan retreat on Abbott Island.

The street names, chosen by the developers, all had some significance. The way to the island commemorated the celebrated temperance advocate John B. Gough, who was scheduled to appear at the Pavilion in 1886. Foss and Abernethy avenues carried the names of the president and secretary of the association. Other streets were named for prominent religious and educational leaders, and still others probably recognized local financial backers.

What happened to the Nebraska Sunday-School Assembly? How can this story be used as a model for investigating the street pattern and plan of any American community? What other types of sources would one normally use in research of this type? What general advice might this example offer for making sense of public places? The time has come to leave the specific example and make some general suggestions for the interpretation of community plans.

Town Plans: Research and Interpretation

The public nature of any particular building, monument, or structure becomes clear by placing it in the context of the community's total plan. These plans usually have their origins as private ventures, similar to the Nebraska Sunday-School Assembly. As a development prospers and matures, it attracts other projects, businesses, and institutions. The final result is a city sewn together like a crazy quilt from a variety of individual efforts. Geography, water courses, the original system of land survey, and the transportation network have usually shaped these diverse individual pieces into an urban fabric with a distinctive design. At various times, especially after the 1890s, formal city planning efforts and comprehensive zoning laws tried to direct the nature and character of a community's physical appearance—to provide, as it were, a master plan.

Building codes, technological developments, public health considerations, economic pressures, and changes in public attitudes have all played roles in shaping the structure of contemporary communities. Each individual building and lot, as it acknowledges these factors, pays homage to decisions made in the past. An important dimension of public places is, therefore, the town plan. These plans were never static but constantly changed over time. Studying a sequence of large-scale maps is the best way to trace the evolution of a community's physical layout. Thus the usual list of suggestions for interpretation concentrates on a variety of cartographic resources.

It is usually easy to locate an old map of the community and then to compare it to a contemporary map available from the local gas station, the planning department at city hall, or the local telephone book. Placing the two maps side by side will provide a "then and now" perspective, but to illustrate the process whereby one plan has evolved into the other, the pair must be supplemented by other maps, dating between the "then" and the "now" documents.

Where can one find these maps? Each community, of course, has its own particular resources for a cartographic history, but one should consider four basic types of large-scale maps usually available for most American communities.

General Land Office Maps

The earliest large-scale maps for the area around Crete, Nebraska, and every other part of the Midwest, are the manuscript maps produced from the original field sketches made by surveyors from the federal land office prior to the sale of the land. These maps, with accompanying notes, are available, in most cases, on microfilm from the state or federal archives. They are the fundamental maps on which many later maps of American communities were based. Figure 3-2 shows such a map for Niles Township in northeastern Illinois.

It takes a keen eye and some effort to use these maps, but they provide an initial benchmark for the history of any community built on property surveyed under the Congressional land system of townships and sections. The original maps are often not in very good condition, and the microfilming process seldom clarifies the documents. The best way to make one of these maps usable is to redraw it as in figure 3-3. In this case, the researcher, in order to make a map of Skokie, Illinois, more meaningful, added cultural

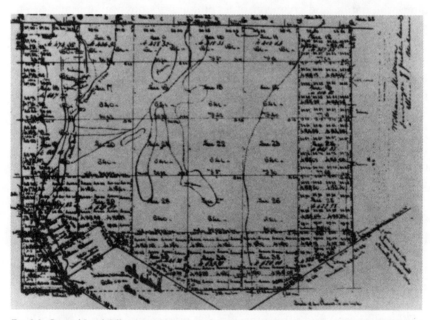

Fig. 3-2. General Land Office Map: Niles Township, Illinois. Before this area of northeastern Illinois was surveyed in the 1830s, certain tracts of land had been set aside as Indian reserves according to the treaties. The pattern of these tracts breaks up the grid-iron pattern of the Congressional survey.

data from other sources. Note how the early pioneer trails and the modern streets and highways help present-day readers orient themselves to the map. The cartographer has also indicated the locations of several contemporary landmarks.

The original surveyors carefully divided the township into sections, although in the Skokie example, the top row of sections was squeezed out by an irregularity in the master plan for surveying this part of northern Illinois. The curvature of the earth, the limitations of the instruments used, and sometimes just plain mistakes by the surveyors produced many such irregularities in the pattern of land division. The division of the township into sections, usually measuring a mile on each side, makes it easy to compare these early maps with later examples. Many nineteenth-century maps used these same reference features and called attention to the fact by including the words "sectional" or "township" in their titles.

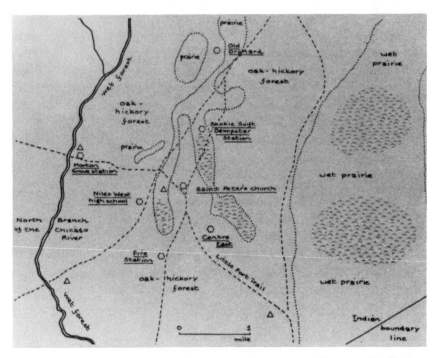

Fig. 3-3. The Niles Township Area, c. 1830. This modern map by Dr. David Buisseret of the Newberry Library of Chicago takes essential information off the land office map and combines it with additional data from other old maps. Several modern landmarks are placed on the map to orient the viewer.

One other irregularity, occasionally found on land office maps, is clearly shown on the Skokie map. The tracts of land at the lower left-hand corner of the map were reserved by Native Americans for their own use or were given away by the federal government to satisfy some type of a claim prior to the systematic survey of the land. The land office maps also usually show some early cultural features such as roads, clearings, Indian villages, pioneer cabins, mines, and so on. Their major importance, however, is to show the natural vegetation and the physical setting that existed prior to settlement by people from the Old World.

By definition, the lands surveyed and mapped by the General Land Office were all public lands. Before the land was subdivided into farms and town lots for individual use, it was all public land. The primary act in the founding of American communities, whether urban or rural, was the division of the land into parcels, which were legally named and then transferred to individuals for their personal use. Some of the land, of course, was reserved by the government for public use. In most cases, however, parcels of land like quarter sections or forty-acre tracts were purchased by private interests who then, in their own way, laid out fields and lots, and then dedicated back to the government, for public use, strips of land for roads, parks, schools, and other other civic needs. This is not only a fundamental understanding to be gained when discussing the nature of public places, but it also provides a key link between the General Land Office maps and an initial subdivision map like that provided by the Nebraska Sunday-School Assembly.

Original Plats

Not all of the land in the United States was surveyed and mapped prior to sale by the General Land Office. The original thirteen states, as well as certain others like Kentucky and Tennessee, had their own systems of land division. Other areas inherited earlier boundaries established by French or Spanish laws and grants. Still other tracts of land were reserved by Native Americans and followed tribal decisions about the use and division of the reservation. Thus a great variety of approaches to land division can be found in different parts of the country.

When towns were laid out on these various tracts, however, certain recurring principles and approaches appeared. The original plat for a town, or its initial city plan, almost always has precedents or parallels in similar examples that can be found nearby. Therefore when an original plan, such as the one of the Nebraska Sunday-School Assembly Grounds, is located, the researcher should place it in the context of other communities laid out according to similar principles.

If the community was a town site such as Crete, Nebraska, the researcher would want to find the original plat of the town. A copy of this document probably was recorded in the public records office or with the county recorder of deeds. A check of some basic secondary sources quickly revealed that the town of Crete was first platted in 1870 as Blue River City. (Federal Writers' Project, *Nebraska: A Guide to the Cornhusker State* [New York: Viking, 1939].) The railroad reached the settlement the following year, and the town was incorporated in 1873. In 1872, Doane College was founded in the community, which explains the name of Doane Avenue on the Sunday-School Assembly Grounds. Thomas Doane, the WPA guide informs us, was the superintendent of the Burlington and Missouri River Rail Road. Perhaps the presence of both the college and the railroad explains why Crete was selected as the site for the Nebraska Chautauqua.

Although the original plats can probably be located in the records of Saline County; it is often more convenient to find copies of early town plans in published form. In this case, the *Checklist of Printed Maps of the Middle West to 1900* edited by Robert H. Karrow (14 volumes, Boston: G. K. Hall, 1981) is a very useful tool. Volume 12, on Nebraska, compiled by Helen Brooks, notes that in 1889 the Crete Improvement Company did publish a map, including thirteen views and a nine-paragraph description of the town. A copy of this map is in the collections of the Nebraska Historical Society. Moreover, the *Checklist* notes other detailed maps of Crete issued in 1878, 1884, 1889, 1897, and 1900. To look at the town plan as it developed from map to map would undoubtedly provide a wealth of information and raise a number of important questions.

County Atlas Maps

Several of the early maps of Crete are from county atlases. These atlases appeared roughly between the 1850s and the 1920s and are usually excellent sources for town plans of small and medium-size communities. Note how the county atlas plan of Geneva, Wisconsin, in 1873 (fig. 3-4) distinguishes between the original town and various additions and later subdivisions. It also provides the names and locations of landmark buildings and important public structures. Several of these, like the Seminary and the Walworth County Courthouse, are pictured on other pages in the atlas (figs. 3-5 and 3-6). The view of Kay's Park on Lake Geneva (fig. 3-7) shows the type of summer retreat that the promoters of the Nebraska Sunday-School Assembly had in mind. They took the idea of the seminary and moved it to the summer park.

It would be instructive to compare the plan of the Nebraska Sunday-School Assembly with the example near Lake Geneva and similar efforts elsewhere. Here the various county atlases from different parts of the nation would provide excellent sources of information. A map of the original grounds of the Chautauqua Lake Camp Meeting Association is reproduced in Pauline Fancher's *Chautauqua: Its Architecture and Its People* (Miami: Banyon Books, 1978), and a list of various related assemblies in 1885 appears as an appendix to John H. Vincent's *The Chautauqua Movement* (1885). Neither the

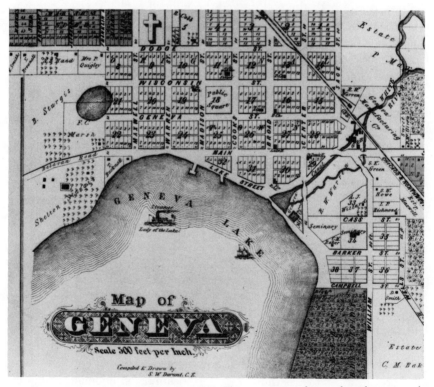

Fig. 3-4. Town Plan of Geneva, Wisconsin, 1873. This is a portion of a map from the county atlas of Walworth County, Wisconsin, published by Everts, Baskin and Stewart of Chicago in 1873. It is typical of the type of map found in these publications. Note how the White River is a source of power for the Geneva Manufacturing Company and how this factory is connected to the railroad.

Fig. 3-5. Lake Geneva Seminary, 1873. The school can be located on the map near the lake in the southern part of the town. The view is, of course, like most county atlas illustrations, somewhat idealized, but the details of the buildings are usually accurate when compared with old photographs or existing structures.

Fig. 3-6. Walworth County Courthouse, 1873. The Walworth County Courthouse was not a very imposing structure in 1873, so the artist dignified the scene by emphasizing the neatness and charm of the landscaping. These details, unlike those of the buildings, were often products of the artist's imagination.

Fig. 3-7. Kay's Park on Lake Geneva, 1873. The summer retreat looks inviting, and the artist has pictured it at the height of activity. The Nebraska Sunday-School Assembly combined this type of a resort facility with a program of educational development and moral uplift.

Crete, Nebraska, assembly nor a similar one established on Lake Geneva appears on the list, but about thirty others are briefly described. Using county atlases, it would be possible to locate additional plans for the communities and to use them to place the Crete map in a comparative perspective.

United States Geological Survey Quadrangles

County maps and atlases provide a systematic cartographic record of rural America in the second half of the nineteenth century. In the twentieth century, the quadrangles published by the United States Geological Survey have a similar function. These detailed topographic maps are part of a national map program: a framework for defense, scientific study, land use, and national resource development. The coverage of the settled parts of the nation is virtually complete, and many communities have been surveyed several times since the 1880s.

The Lincoln, Nebraska, sheet of the preliminary Reconnaissance Map, produced by the United States Geological Survey in 1894 and 1895 (fig. 3-8) clearly shows how the original system of land survey made a grid pattern of the land. The grounds of the Nebraska Sunday-School Assembly are not indicated on the map, but we can surmise, by the loop in the river, that the site was located next to the town on the north and west sides immediately across the stream. The town plan, in contrast to the plan of the Assem-

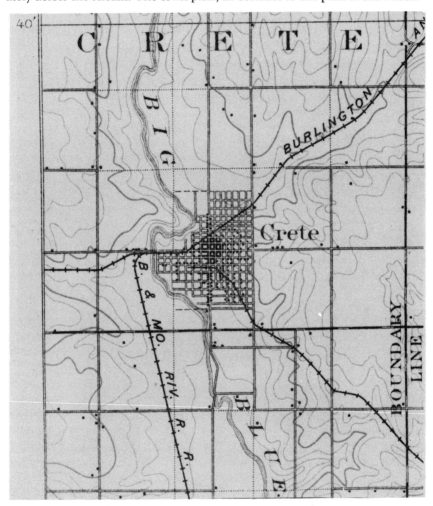

Fig. 3-8. Crete, Nebraska, on a Topographical Map from 1894-1895. This is a portion of the Lincoln, Nebraska, sheet of the preliminary reconnaissance map issued by the United States Geological Survey in 1895. The rectangular pattern of the streets and roads contrasts with the course of the river and the routes used by the railroads.

bly Grounds, rigidly follows the section lines. The only major cultural features
to disregard the rectangular survey are the railroads, which tended to take
the shortest and most convenient routes across the prairie.

A later survey by the United States Geological Survey (fig. 3-9) was based
on aerial photographs taken in 1962 and then field-checked in 1964. The
map uses a larger scale and shows more detail, but the town of Crete now
appears at the edge of the quadrangle. Two different sheets, Crete North
and Crete South, are needed to note the full extent of the changes in the
town plan wrought by the automobile. The new maps conveniently label
the sections of the township and number the highways.

The quadrangles from the 1960s provide many more details because of

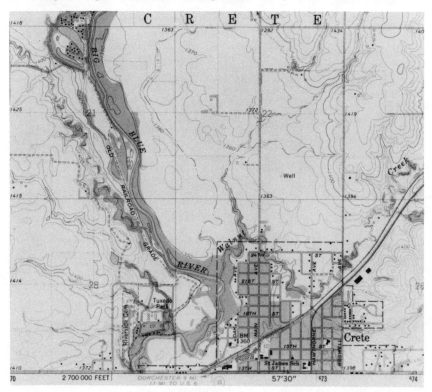

Fig. 3-9. Crete, Nebraska, on a Topographic Map from 1964. The Crete North quadrangle map produced
by the United States Geological Survey in 1964 uses a much larger scale than the 1895 map. Thus
it is possible to include more data and to trace the imprint of the old Nebraska Sunday-School Assembly grounds. By comparing the 1895 and 1964 maps, one can readily make a list of changes, but the
continuity of the town plan is equally worthy of note.

the enlarged scale. We can see that the old Sunday-School Assembly Grounds were still devoted to recreational purposes. Tuxedo Park in 1964 apparently used some traces of the old road system for the grounds. The grassy area of Woodlawn Park still shows up on the map, and the bridge over the river seems to be in about the same location. The map even indicates a building on the site of the old hotel. Abbott Island, however, has disappeared with a shift in course of the Big Blue River, an oxbow lake taking its place.

Outside the town, one can note the new state highway alongside the railroad tracks. Crete also extended a bit to the east with a new subdivision, but there was no expansion to the north. The 1972 revision of this map shows the continued building of homes on the curved streets in the new subdivision, and new factories or warehouses appeared along the highway out of town. Several new buildings also were erected in Tuxedo Park near the site of the old hotel. The basic plan of Crete, however, records very few changes. Like the topography and the general course of the river, it provides a constant frame of reference as we proceed from map to map.

The town plan expresses the continuity of American history. Major changes, like the use of the automobile, transformed the way people lived in Crete between the 1890s and the 1970s, but the result was only a slight modification of the basic urban structure. Tuxedo Park does not exactly duplicate the Sunday-School Assembly, but the general land-use classification remains much the same. Public survey of the land, private routing of the railroad and platting of the town, and then public incorporation of the community as a legal entity in the 1870s created an enduring plan for Crete that has remained intact for a century and will probably endure for years to come.

Suggested Readings

The best way to begin further study of the history of a town plan is to assemble a similar set of maps as far as they are available for the community of interest:

1. Before there was a town—the Land Office survey (state archives)
2. Original town plats (county records)
3. Latter town plans (county atlases)
4. Twentieth-century developments (various editions of the USGS quadrangles)

A prototype for this type of effort is *Skokie: A Community History Using Old Maps* by David Buisseret and Gerald Danzer (Chicago: Skokie Historical Society and the Newberry Library, 1985). It places sixteen different maps and aerial photographs in chronological order and then provides drawings and extensive notes to re-create the historical geography of a Chicago suburb. A manual on how historians might use old maps is currently being prepared by David Buisseret at the Smith Center for the History of Cartography at the Newberry Library. Anyone who wishes to look at a particular map from all possible angles might profit by the outline of suggestions for using maps as primary sources in Appendix B, "Working with Space."

The leading authority on American county atlases is Michael Conzen at the University of Chicago. He has published a variety of articles on the subject, but his full-length discussion with a union list of the atlases is still to come. Some states already have useful introductions to state and local maps. A model is *Windows to the Past: A Bibliography of Minnesota County Atlases* by Mai Treude (Minneapolis: Center for Urban and Regional Affairs, 1980), which has a helpful introduction.

The best guide to interpreting the USGS quadrangles is the *Atlas of Cultural Features* by Benjamin F. Richason (Chicago: Hubbard Press, 1972). This "study of man's imprint on the land" gives portions of topographic sheets on one page and provides an aerial photograph and commentary on the opposite page. The USGS quadrangles should always be used with the guide sheet of topographic symbols at hand, but remember that some variations appear on the older maps. Current maps are available at a reasonable price from the United States Geological Survey, Map Distribution, Box 25286, Federal Center, Denver, Colorado 80225. Be sure to consult the index map for your state so you will know the name of the appropriate quadrangle. These index maps are available at local libraries or from the address listed above. Riley Moore Moffat has compiled a *Map Index to Topographic Quadrangles of the United States, 1882-1940* (Santa Cruz, Calif.: Western Association of Map Libraries, 1986).

The standard work on the history of city planning in the United States, based on the plans themselves, is *The Making of Urban America* by John W. Reps (Princeton: Princeton University Press, 1965). It does not cover the twentieth century, but it does provide illustrations of some 300 plans and extensive commentaries on those of particular significance. A subsequent work by Reps, *Cities of the American West: A History of Frontier Urban Planning* (Princeton: Princeton University Press, 1979) is particularly good on the impact of railroads on town plans. A more compact version of the same information may be found in his *The Forgotten Frontier: Urban Planning in the American West before 1890* (Columbia: University of Missouri Press, 1981).

The best book to help a beginner look at a town plan, or the town itself in real life, is Grady Clay's *Close Up: How to Read the American City* (Chicago: University of Chicago Press, 1973). Each chapter in this book focuses on one aspect of the cityscape, and for each of these, the author has coined a name: fixes, epitome districts, fronts, strips, beats, stocks, sinks, turf, and vantages. Each concept is then explained in the text, richly supplemented by maps, plans, photographs, and drawings.

For an introduction to the work of professional city planners, a good place to start would be with the *Proceedings of the Fifth National Conference on City Planning* (Boston, 1913). The conference sponsored a contest to design the best subdivision for a particular site. The *Proceedings* reprints nine of the entries and then provides detailed commentaries and comparative analyses.

John R. Stilgoe's masterly presentation of the *Common Landscape of America, 1580 to*

1845 (New Haven, Conn.: Yale University Press, 1982) is the best introduction to the look of early American communities. The study is based on printed sources and field investigations rather than maps, so it will require a leap of imagination to apply Stilgoe's insight to a particular town plan. Once the leap has been made, however, one's conception of the landscapes, town plans, and even history itself will be transformed.

Finally, we return to the story of the Nebraska Assembly. It underscores how the interpretation of primary sources, in general, and maps, in particular, should always be done in the context of secondary sources as well. After the analysis of the map was made, the author was able to locate a copy of *Pioneer Days in Crete, Nebraska*, privately printed in Chadron, Nebraska in 1937. The author, Annadora Foss Gregory, a descendant of one of the Assembly's founders, produced a magnificent and detailed study of the town and the Assembly, documenting most of our conclusions. Although aware that 75,000 copies of the map stationery had been printed, she apparently did not have a copy at her disposal. Such is often the fate of ephemeral items. The copy the author discovered at a flea market is now in the Newberry Library in Chicago.

·4·

Streets

THE PLAN OF A TOWN OR A CITY IS ALWAYS FASHIONED by laying out its streets. These public ways perform two initial functions: they divide the community into blocks or parcels, and they relate the individual pieces of land to each other and to the community as a whole. Streets create boundaries but, at the same time, engender social contact and make possible a civic life. In both instances, they perform fundamental public functions.

A careful look at the streets of a community will tell an observer much more than documenting this philosophical premise. In more tangible ways, streets can be seen as meeting places, playgrounds, and parade grounds. They reveal the social and cultural life of the neighborhood: its music, art, and even its poetry and prose. Sometimes they serve as marketplaces or commercial centers. At other times, they are almost entirely devoted to their primary functions as transportation and communication arteries. At all times, however, they record technological and cultural change. Depending on the point of view, streets may be seen as showcases of modern technology, as remnants of a past way of life, as galleries for viewing architectural treasures, as botanical collections, as parking lots, or as garbage bins.

Roads may be thought of as rural counterparts to urban streets. On a map like the Crete Quadrangle (fig. 3-9), the streets of a community are grouped together and react to one another. The roads, on the other hand, seem more distant and more reserved. Of course they perform the same basic functions as the town streets, they divide properties, and they connect one tract of land with all of the others. Good roads were always considered an essential means of creating a rural community out of a group of farms.

A road connects a town with its rural hinterland. If a road goes beyond
that and connects one community with another, we are apt to call it a "highway." As the importance of the highway increases, it grows in size and in
the amount of services society provides for its travelers. Maps usually record
these different types of highways, roads, and streets by using various lines,
symbols, and colors. At the same time, however, transportation maps show
how all of the public ways are connected to each other and emphasize how
they create, as an ensemble, the pattern of community life.

Post Cards of Main Street

Maps are certainly essential to the study of a community's streets and roads,
but they tend to be fairly abstract for our purpose, to see the street as a public place. Pictures might be a better source to consider in this chapter, and
what source would be better than post cards of Main Street? Nearly every
American town large enough to attract visitors in the first half of the twentieth century provided post cards of its major streetscape for visitors to send
to the folks back home. As thousands of collectors have discovered, old post
cards provide an interesting and instructive window to the past. They are
readily available, inexpensive, and easy to store. They provide a rich resource
for doing many types of nearby history, and they demonstrate so well the
nature of the street as a public place.

Each of the six post cards reproduced in this chapter portrays a portion
of a Main Street between 1906 and 1926, two decades that witnessed the·
advent of the automobile as a fixture on the nation's streets. Our discussion
of each view includes four general categories:

- •the buildings, their architecture and their functions
- •the vehicles on the streets
- •the people in the view
- •the street itself, its paving and its furnishings.

The post card of Main Street in Hunter, North Dakota (fig. 4-1), in the
Red River Valley of the North, was mailed in 1908. The photograph itself
is not dated, but the back of the card informs us that it was made by L.
A. Foster Photo Company of Kewanee, Illinois. The scene looks like a tran-
quil morning view. The man on the left, perhaps even the owner of the
store, Knudtson himself, is washing the store window in preparation for a
day of activity. A woman down the street, probably another shopkeeper,

Fig. 4-1. Main Street, Hunter, North Dakota, c. 1908. A broad Main Street was sometimes explained as an accommodation for cattle drives. Located in the wheat belt, Hunter seems to have been laid out with a broad avenue down the center.

checks the scene, while a few early arrivals seem to be waiting for the day's activities to begin. Only one vehicle, a horse-drawn buggy, appears on the street.

The wooden sidewalk is elevated to accommodate passengers alighting from wagons and buggies. The street itself, reached by a ramp or stairs, is graded but unpaved. Note how the wooden sidewalk continues across the street for the comfort of pedestrians. It looks as though the wooden pathway in the street had just been shoveled clean before the photograph was taken, an early example of the town's concern for its public image. Several street lamps on top of wooden posts, a taller pole of undetermined function beside the buggy, and several hitching posts complete the street furniture.

The buildings present an arresting streetscape. Although modest in size, they sport some interesting decorations above the cornice line and give the facade of the street an interesting rhythm. Knudtson, who must have paid the photographer to come to town, obviously has a fine store selling general merchandise. Down the block, the larger store with the woman in the doorway might have been his major competitor.

The quiet scene in Hunter contrasts sharply the bustle of activity in Pueblo, Colorado (fig. 4-2). This view of Main Street shows a major commercial thoroughfare in a much larger community at the height of business activity.

Fig. 4-2. Main Street, Pueblo, Colorado, c. 1910. A view from the highest point in a city has always had a peculiar attraction. This perspective seems to give one a sense of control over the urban environment. At the same time, one seems to be close enough in this roof-top perspective to participate in the activities of the street below.

The buildings are much more substantial structures, the tall ones in the background obviously needing elevators. The high buildings and the crowd of people made public transportation a necessity.

The three streetcars and the tracks down the center of the street dominate the scene and explain why; in referring to this period, historians often use the phrase "streetcar cities." The streetcars were powered by electric motors, which received their current from a trolley wire hung above the street. The trolley wires, in turn, were supported by cross wires suspended between the tall poles appearing at regular intervals on each side of the street. The horse-drawn carts, wagons, and buggies all seem to stay at a respectful distance from the streetcar tracks.

The people in the view appear to be lining the street in anticipation of a parade. The fact that no vehicles are parked at the curbs supports this hypothesis, as do the few heads beginning to appear in the upper story windows.

The large building on the left is a fine example of commercial architecture in the streetcar city. Although it reached five stories in height, this structure may not have had elevator service. Four or five stories was the usual limit for walk-up buildings. The front of the structure facing Main Street is designed so that each story has its own individual character. The special treatment of the vertical center of the facade, with columns, bays, and an arch at the top, gives the building visual interest and also ties the various stories together. A pedestrian observing this structure would find a great deal of visual interest.

One should remember that every commuter on a streetcar was a pedestrian at both ends of the ride. Streetcars, a concern for the needs of pedestrians, and architectural variety often went hand-in-hand. When cities discarded the streetcars, the other characteristics often seemed to be lost as well.

The 1907 view of North Main Street in Providence, Rhode Island, seems to document this observation (fig. 4-3). Here we have a pedestrian's perspective on the streetscape. The view looks like a room with walls of four- and five-story buildings presenting a great variety of textures and designs.

Fig. 4-3. Main Street, Providence, Rhode Island, c. 1907. The awnings on the buildings not only served a very essential function on a hot summer day, but they also seemed to extend the structures into the street, connecting them with the public space.

But the people boarding and leaving the streetcars and walking from store to store do not seem to notice the splendor surrounding them. A boy on the stoop to the right seems to be the only one taking in the full impact of the display.

A close inspection of the view reveals that the buildings were used for more than stores. Offices of the Mercantile Trust Company and space for a printing establishment occupy the building on the right with the arched windows along the second story. The streets, like the buildings, served a variety of needs: streetcars, horse-drawn vehicles, and pedestrians all used the public way according to their own purposes.

The variety of activities in a public way is also apparent in the view of Main Street in Staunton, Virginia, about 1910 (fig. 4-4). One set of tracks down the center of the street and the absence of trolley wires or poles suggest that the tracks were used by a steam-powered railroad. Or, since horse-drawn vehicles seem to be the usual form of transportation in the view, perhaps the tracks served an old horse-car line. The narrow street might pose problems in trying to accommodate the newfangled automobiles, but in this scene, the restricted space seems to help people relate to each other. Notice how some shops have extended their awnings over the whole sidewalk and supported them with poles at the curbside. Also note how the group of people at the right is posing for the photographer. Each building lining the street also seems to relate to its neighbors across the way and down the block. At the same time, each structure has its own character and decor.

The variety of signs in the view are good clues to the social and economic life of the block. Using a magnifying glass, an essential tool when using photographs as primary sources, one can identify the Beverly Book Company, which sold "books, stationery, and office supplies." Two dry goods stores, a pair of shoe stores, an ice cream parlor, and a store selling pianos and organs also can be identified by their signs.

The post card of Tucumcari, New Mexico (fig. 4-5), shows Main Street at a slightly later date and with a much different character. Probably dating from the 1920s, the card suggests that automobiles have taken over the street. Pedestrians now cross only at corners and only when the street is clear of traffic. The street light is suspended in the middle of the intersection to provide more light for the benefit of the cars but at some cost to the pedestrians. The street seems to be paved; perhaps it is in even better shape than the sidewalks.

As a whole, this view of Main Street seems to celebrate the social or cul-

Fig. 4-4. Main Street, Staunton, Virginia, c. 1910. It might be reasonable to assume that the width of this street was set by a much earlier pattern of land use. As the community grew and the business section developed, the width of the street remained the same. By 1910, street-widening campaigns were conducted in many cities.

Fig. 4-5. Main Street, Tucumcari, New Mexico. From today's perspective, this view may seem a bit stark, but at the time, the smoke stacks and water tower were probably hailed as signs of progress. Not only do Main Streets change over time, but so do the attitudes people have toward them.

tural aspects of civic life to a much lesser extent. Some of the newer buildings on the street appear in plain dress, much more functional in appearance,
and provide little visual interest to the passers-by. Cornices are no longer
of great importance now that much of the street has become a parking place
for automobiles. The water tank provides a fitting symbol for the changing
nature and function of the place. Its stark functionalism may be taken as
a sign of progress, along with the horseless carriages lining the street and
the prominent sign locating the electric company.

It is hard to spot signs of big changes on North Main Street in Stoyestown,
Pennsylvania, about a decade earlier (fig. 4-6). The whole scence seems to
be as traditional as the church steeple standing guard over the streetscape.
The public way is being used as a playground by the three small girls at
the left. A close inspection of the card reveals nine or ten other people
posing for the photographer along the sidewalks. The unpaved street is occasionally met by covered walkways so that the buildings seem to interlock
with the thoroughfare.

The banner stretching across the way obviously announces something of

North Main Street, Stoyestown, Pa.

Fig. 4-6. Main Street, Stoyestown, Pennsylvania, c. 1914. The mature trees along the roadside give
this view a very comfortable look. The absence of any traffic increases the sense of peace and quiet.
Most post cards of Main Street, however, tried to emphasize the bustle of commerce or the swelling
population of the community.

importance. A cryptic note on the back of the card simply says, "Stopped at Hight House all night July 11, 1914." A magnifying glass clarifies the issue and invests the post card with significance. It shows that the legend of the banner reads "AUTOMOBILES." Our hypothesis suggests that Stoyestown had prepared for a cross-country automobile race or an excursion by an automobile club. One of the participants recorded his or her stay in the town by purchasing a post card of Main Street and recording the date on the back. The card is also numbered in the same hand but apparently on another occasion. It is "16," and it would be interesting to have other documents in the series. Numbers 1 through 15 might enable us to trace the individual's route and to collect other details of his or her adventure. As it is, the post card helps us document the changing nature of Main Street in the early decades of the century.

The six post cards were selected by a serious post card collector from a file of more than a thousand views of Main Streets. David Wilson simply took a random sampling meeting our requirement of date and a variety of locations and his criteria of an interesting view. The discussion uses a variety of ways to interpret these cards and to invest them with significance. It recognizes Main Street as a public place and focuses on the process of change. We might continue the story with more recent views or more diverse examples, but it is more appropriate to step back from the discussion and make some suggestion for interpreting streets as public places.

Interpreting Streets

Issues. The first suggestion is to be alert to the formation of political issues when interpreting streets and roads. As public places in the most basic sense of the word, streets were the sites of activities relating to many of the political questions of the past. Using a magnifying glass, it is possible to see, on several Main Street post cards, handbills and posters advocating candidates and their platforms. Streets traditionally were places for political rallies, parades, and soapbox oratory. The selling of newspapers, as an exchange of opinion and as the expression of free speech, has long been a sanctioned activity on the streets.

But the connection between a public way and the issues of the day go beyond its use as a forum. The laying out of the streets, as we have seen, was as fundamental to the building of a town as securing its charter. The improvement and maintenance of these thoroughfares was always a matter of debate among the voters. How much should the public be taxed to support the roadways?

As citizens demanded additional services from their local governments, the streets were the means by which these benefits reached individual lots and citizens. Streets became vehicles for water supply, police and fire protection, sewers, garbage collection, and utilities of all kinds. The rise of public parks in the nineteenth century was also closely connected with the development of parkways and boulevards, special streets that provided citizens with appropriate leisure-time activities. The chartering of private companies to provide streetcar service, gas, water, and steam for heating raised matters for discussion: To what extent could public ways be used for private benefit? How much should the public be inconvenienced as the streets were torn up and equipped to provide these services? If the public ways were used for private gain, should not the rates and the profits of these enterprises be regulated? In the process of discussion, the modern concept of local government emerged, and the streets were transformed.

The discussion of the six post cards illuminates another perspective on this revolution in the public ways. It centers on the advent of the automobile city, where streets were largely given over to the new horseless carriages. With the loss of a multifaceted street life, communities became, like their primary mode of transportation, more private and less public.

A decline in civic consciousness, critics explained, accompanies the loss of street-based activities. The original streets, John Brinckerhoff Jackson explained, "were made for any and every kind of outdoor group activity, from children's games to funeral processions and endless loitering in the sun. All civic architecture is essentially nothing but an appropriate background for this life; and city planning is chiefly justified when it helps preserve and foster informal community activities" (*Landscapes: Selected Writings* [Amherst: University of Massachusetts Press, 1970], p. 111). Jackson's standards provide a stern test for many political decisions of the last decades and could inform a historical account of any street in the nation.

The argument about streets, however, should not be considered something that emerged after expressways cut through the cities and interstate highways traversed the continent. Frank Lloyd Wright, the well-known architect, told reporters in 1925 that the automobile was going to ruin the city. Michigan Avenue in Chicago, he declared, was no longer a boulevard. "It's a race track! This is a dreadful way to live. You'll be strangled by traffic." In answering the inevitable question about what could be done to head off the disaster, the architect's reply focused on buildings rather than the streets: "Take a giant knife and sweep it over the Loop, cutting off every building at the seventh floor. If you cut down those horrible buildings, you'll have no traffic jams. You'll have trees again. You'll have some joy in the life of this city. After all, that is the job of the architect—to give the world a little joy" (from Finis Farr's *Chicago* [New Rochelle, N.Y.: Arlington House, 1973], p. 355).

Buildings. The buildings lining the street, in Jackson's view, performed a civic function by providing an appropriate backdrop for informal social contact among the citizens. Architects and developers often stake out much more aggressive claims for their structures. But all parties agree that the history of a street is largely the story of the buildings erected along its right-of-way.

The relationships between these structures and the life of the street can be pursued by using a variety of approaches: architectural style, date of construction, the materials and techniques used, the function of the buildings, and the particular people who used them. The important factor, however, is to see the buildings as an ensemble on the block or as part of a continuum down the street, across the town, and even out into the countryside. There are many books on the aesthetic dimension of the streetscape, but few guidebooks point out the economic, social, technological, or cultural ties between buildings on a street.

The interpretive patterns often do not work out completely on one individual street. One morning, I drove through several towns in the dairy belt of southwestern Wisconsin and tried to line up five related buildings on one street. The best I could do was (1) a dairy barn at the edge of town, (2) a gasoline station, (3) a bank, (4) a cheese factory, and (5) an agricultural implement store. I discovered this pattern in nearly half of the towns I visited. Thinking about the ways in which these structures are related encourages us to see the links between buildings and the street and then to realize how they are joined in an alliance made possible by the public way. The cheese factory depends on the dairy farms for its supply of milk. The farmers in turn need tools and fuel to provide the milk. The bank provides the financing and the monetary transfers that support the interaction between the various individual citizens and their buildings.

Vehicles. The simple enumeration of various types of vehicles in the post card views of Main Street alerted us to its changing nature and use. An inventory of the automobiles parked along a residential street might provide evidence for the economic status of the neighborhood or its social aspirations. A list of the type of trucks making deliveries and pick-ups on a block would make an interesting social document if the study extended over a long enough period of time or had some comparative basis.

A social history of a residential street could be developed around the vehicles using it over the years: the ice wagon, the ragman's cart, the coal truck, the milk truck, the camper, and the moped. Another approach would be to relate the street furnishings to different types of vehicles at different periods in the life of the street. Hitching posts and water troughs belong to one era; parking meters and yellow painted curbs belong to another.

The story of the garage provides another interesting commentary on the emergence of the automobile as the primary force shaping the residential street in the twentieth century. In the early decades, owners needed to cover their automobiles or provide a special building for them. These garages, a name derived from the French verb "to protect or preserve," were considered utility sheds and consigned to the rear of the lots. They could be reached only by alleys or long driveways. By the middle of the century, new suburban developments brought the garage up alongside the house and then connected the two structures with a breezeway.

After a few years, the garage expanded in size, moved into the house, and took the most prominent place at the front of the property. The garage door then became the focal point of a home, and owners often lavished special attention on its decoration. Some commentators have noted that with the arrival of the garage in the place of honor in the new suburbs, sidewalks were sometimes banished. The absence of sidewalks took the private city to its extreme, dividing the community into private lots and streets designed for private vehicles. In these communities, streets almost entirely lost their social function and became merely utility corridors and passageways.

Utilities. The history of a street can often be outlined by noting the appearance of various services and utilities. A chronology or a time line recording these developments opens up some avenues to its interpretation. When did streetcars first operate on State Street? When was it paved? In what year did it get street lights? When did telephone wires appear? Where was the first traffic light or special lane for left turns? When was the last time that State Street was closed to all vehicular traffic and for what purpose? When are the utility wires scheduled to be placed underground for aesthetic reasons?

Not all of these questions are answered by the chronology of Peachtree Street, 1855-1885, provided in figure 4-7, but one can read between the lines, or the dates, and sense the changes taking place in both the rhythms of everyday life and in the role of government. Extending the chronology up to the present would amplify the point, but no one should underestimate the time and resourcefulness needed to develop such a time line. The city department of streets might have records to help continue the list, but such is not often the case. The various public utilities can supply some key dates for the development of their respective systems, dates that then can be fleshed out by consulting contemporaneous newspaper accounts. In the case of major improvements, the annual reports of various utilities and governmental departments are often invaluable.

Because the introduction of utility service was always hailed as a sign of progress, the buildings that were erected to house the administrative functions of a public gas, electric, or water system often took on the elaborate architectural style of a major civic showcase. The office buildings erected by the public utilities in the early years of the twentieth century are often among the most elaborate structures in the central business district (fig. 4-8). Their splendid facades, encrusted with ornamental cornices, colonnades,

A Street is Furnished:
Peachtree Street, Atlanta

1855 — Gaslighting system installed
1870 — Garbage collection begun. Laws regulating the placing of garbage on the street enacted.
1871-1872 — First street railway.
1873 — Full-time police service.
1873 — Free mail delivery.
1873 — Standardized numbering system instituted.
1875 — Waterworks system installed.
1875 — First fire hydrants.
1879 — First telephone service.
1882 — Portion of Peachtree Street paved.
1885 — New water system.
1885 — Granite sidewalks installed.
1885 — Electric lights initiated.

Fig. 4-7. The data was gathered from William Bailey Williford, *Peachtree Street, Atlanta* (Athens: University of Georgia Press, 1962).

Fig. 4-8. Gas and Electric Building at Night, Denver, Colorado, c. 1920. This ornate office building for a public utility advertised itself as "the best lighted building in the world." Today consumers would inquire who was paying for this expensive display, but in the 1920s such efforts were often applauded as an honor to civic pride.

and royal finery, supposedly reflected the triumph of the democratic way. In the New Era, so the argument went, technology had made every man a prince, every woman a princess, and every house a showcase of progress. It was, therefore, appropriate that the Edison Building, the offices of People's Gas, or the building for the Water Department resemble a palace. The conduits, pipes, and wires above, alongside, and under the streets were often pictured like an army of progress, helping each citizen to be more fully engaged in the pursuit of happiness.

Systems. Like the streets themselves, the utility structures are incomplete unless seen as parts of a system. The interpretive jump from part to whole is, as we have seen, a key element in grasping the communal nature of public places. To see the system behind the individual object on a street is to realize the organic nature of the community. The utility pole is thus only a part of an electric power grid or a telephone system. The hydrant marks the presence of a network of pipes bringing pure water to every home and the availability of special equipment and personnel to convert this water supply into a fire-fighting mechanism. The sewer cover indicates the silent presence of drainage or sanitation facilities to take the waste water away.

Several graphic aids are of great use in helping people read the street in the context of systems, to see it as a conduit for more than traffic, and to grasp more fully the public or communal nature of the passageway. The cross section helps one visualize how a thoroughfare extends above and below the surface. The air above the street was recognized, from an early date, as a public resource providing light and fresh air. The height and shape of buildings lining the street could therefore be regulated by ordinances to protect this natural resource. Below grade, a cross section of the street usually reveals a variety of pipes and drains providing essential services. On occasion, subways for mass transit, for the movement of goods, or for the use of pedestrians have been built in congested areas, thus providing, like elevated railways above the street, for various levels and modes of conveyance (fig. 4-9). Even the most simple roadway, viewed in cross section, becomes a complicated pattern of subsurface, pavement, arrangements for drainage, the distribution of utilities, and so on.

A second essential graphic device for interpreting a particular street as a system of utilities is a map drawn to show the location of the major elements in a particular network. A map of the water supply, for example, would show the source of the water supply, the facilities for storing it or for trans-

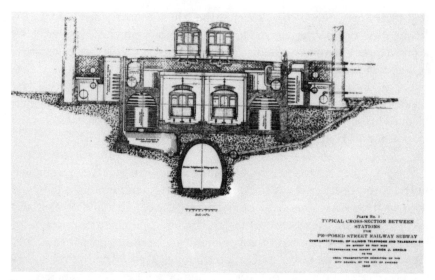

Fig. 4-9. Cross-Section of an Urban Street. This drawing shows a typical street in the congested central business district of an early twentieth-century city. It extends from building to building and shows a whole network of pipes and drains beneath the sidewalks. Streetcars were the major form of urban transportation at this time. From Bion J. Arnold's, *Report on the Engineering and Operating Features of the Chicago Transportation Problem* (1902).

porting it to the city, the plant for purifying the water, the pumps used to move the water through the mains, and the network of pipes for distribution to the public. Water towers or stand pipes to provide even pressure, various control devices, mechanisms for ensuring water quality, and an administrative building also might be located on the map. Different symbols, colors, or lines might be used to distinguish different types and sizes of water mains: major trunk lines, branches, feeders, and local distribution pipes. The map will thus clarify the variety of mechanisms needed to make a water system function.

A third type of graphic device, the chart, might clarify the elements of a system or indicate how one utility is related to the others. A water supply system also needs a water disposal system. After use for drinking, cooking, washing, and so on, the water must be taken away, purified, and returned to nature. Moreover, the pumps used to provide the water pressure need a power source: electricity in modern cities but usually steam from burning wood, coal, or gas in an earlier period. The use of water for home cooking or washing also depends on a system for heating it, with energy supplied perhaps by gas or electricity. The chart might include the necessity of the telephone or the mail as communication devices essential to the functioning of large systems. In the end, it will reveal that the street, like the community itself, is really a system of systems.

Suggested Readings

Bernard Rudofsky, writing in 1969, claimed that no book had then been written on the American street, its nature or its history. He redressed the situation with *Streets for People: A Primer for Americans* (Garden City, N.Y.: Anchor, 1969), a ringing appeal to fight for the pedestrian's rights to the nation's streets. The book has as many illustrations as it does text, and most of these show Old World examples. Despite its polemical tone, it is still worthwhile to start any research project involving a street by paging through this volume and reading carefully chapter 6, "The Street is Where the Action Is."

Two additional writers who greatly influenced the discussion in the 1960s on the nature of cities and their street life were Lewis Mumford and Jane Jacobs. Mumford's two dozen books on the built environment go back to the 1920s and are always worth consulting, but if one needs an introduction, the best place to start is probably his *The Urban Prospect* (New York: Harcourt, Brace and World, 1968), especially chapter 6, "The Highway and the City." Jane Jacobs began her classic book on *The Death and Life of Great American Cities* (New York: Random House, 1961) with three chapters on the uses of sidewalks: for safety, for contact, and for assimilating children.

The focus on Main Street as a historical environment where one can "see urban history" was suggested by Carole Rifkind's *Main Street: The Face of Urban America* (New York: Harper and Row, 1977). Most of the book is devoted to the analysis of photographs. A stimulating aspect of the study is its organization into four general categories: "origins," "structure," "experience," and "change." The wide-ranging bibliography should not be overlooked. Rifkind's book may well serve as a handbook for creating museum exhibits focusing on Main Streets in cities and towns across the nation. One such effort, with a published catalogue, is "Main Street: Mirror of Change" (1980), mounted by The Kentucky Museum at Western Kentucky University in Bowling Green. Lewis Atherton's *Main Street on the Middle Border* (Bloomington: Indiana University Press, 1954) combs documentary materials to make many keen observations about Main Street as the matrix of the American character.

The use of post cards as historical sources has not developed as fully as the rage for collecting these charming documents of American popular taste. There is a voluminous literature on post cards written for collectors, including *Picture Postcards in the United States, 1893-1918* (New York: Clarkson N. Potter, 1976) by George and Dorothy Miller. Dover Publications of New York has also issued booklets of post cards with old views for various cities. These are often photographs reproduced as post cards rather than reprints of original post card views. A more extended treatment of *Chicago at the Turn of the Century in Photographs*, by Larry A. Viskochil (New York: Dover, 1984) is based on the original negatives from which post cards were made, often with alterations.

For the interpretation of old photographs of American cities, the most complete study is *Silver Cities: The Photography of American Urbanization, 1839-1915* (Philadelphia: Temple University Press, 1984) by Peter Bacon Hales. He builds a very useful analysis by looking at the pictures in three ways: at their subject matter as a source of information, at their symbolic content for their celebratory message, and at their composition as an artistic statement.

Although there still is no comprehensive history of the street in America, roads and highways have received a great deal of attention, and much of this literature can be used by the historian of the street. One of the most recent of these studies, and one of the most helpful for a beginning student, is *U.S. 40: A Roadscape of the American Experience* by Thomas J. Schlereth (Indianapolis: Indiana Historical Society, 1985). Its first section, "Reading the Road: The Above-Ground Archaeology of the American Highway" is a primer on how beginning students can use the landscape as a historical source. Part II of Schlereth's study focuses on the section of the highway that crosses Indiana. Part III, "The Road in American Life—Selected Sources," is the best bibliographical essay on the topic and should be consulted by every student.

The vehicles on the streets in old views can be identified by using Jack D. Rittenhouse's *American Horse-Drawn Vehicles* (New York: Bonanza Books, 1948), a collection of 218 pictures. There are several excellent studies on the impact of the automobile on American life, all published by MIT Press in Cambridge, Massachusetts: *America Adopts the Automobile, 1895-1910* (1970) by James Flink; *The Car Culture* (1975) by the same author; and *The Road and the Car in American Life* (1971) by John B. Rae. In addition, I would recommend looking at one readily available primary source, *Planning for City Traffic* (1927), a collection of studies edited by Austin MacDonald and issued as volume 133 in *The Annals of the American Academy of Political and Social Science*. One interesting chapter suggests different types of street lights for different social and economic districts in the city. Another analyzes traffic accidents and recommends the use of stop-and-go signals placed "in the path of traffic."

On the streets as corridors for public utilities, one should consult the various publications issued by and sold through the Public Works Historical Society. Volume 14 of its *Essays in Public Works History*, for example, contains three articles on *Infrastructure and Urban Growth in the Nineteenth Century* (Chicago, 1985). *Public Works History in the United States*, a bibliography edited by Suellen M. Hoy and Michael C. Robinson (Nashville: American Association for State and Local History, 1981) has a section on roads and streets.

One of the best studies focusing on a particular city uses the development of streets and utilities as its central theme: Harold L. Platt's *City Building in the New South: The Growth of Public Services in Houston, Texas, 1830-1910* (Philadelphia: Temple University Press, 1983). Readers should pay special attention to the general works cited in Platt's notes, which take the place of a general bibliography.

Several famous streets have been featured in book-length studies, but these are usually popular accounts. One will, however, find many helpful suggestions in such volumes as *Peachtree Street, Atlanta* by William Bailey Williford (Athens: University of Georgia Press, 1962) or older works like *The Greatest Street in the World* by Stephen Jenkins (New York: Putnam's Sons, 1911), "the story of Broadway, Old and New, from the Bowling Green to Albany." Additional information on the rhythms of the street life in the metropolis can be found in the "light and darkness" books published in the latter part of the nineteenth century to tell rural folks about life in the teeming metropolis. Broadway, for example, is discussed in *Lights and Shadows of New York* by James D. McCabe (Philadelphia: National Publishing Company, 1879), *New York by Sunlight and Gaslight* by the same author (Cincinnati: Jones Brothers, 1882), and *Darkness and Daylight; or Lights and Shadows of New York* by Helen Campbell and others (Hartford, Conn.: Hartford Publishing Company, 1895).

Our discussion has tended to emphasize the nineteenth and twentieth centuries. For streets in early America, much valuable information can be gathered from Carol Bridenbaugh's works published by Alfred A. Knopf in New York: *Cities in the the Wilderness: The First Century of Urban Life in America, 1625-1724* (1938) and *Cities in Revolt: Urban Life in America, 1743-1776* (1955). *Colonial Yorktown's Main Street* edited by Charles E. Hatch, Jr. (New York: Eastern National Park and Monument Association, 1980) reprints an earlier study by the National Park Service. It is a detailed and fascinating study and makes the point that this Main Street was dominated by the windmill.

Pushing back still further in time to the street patterns of medieval European villages that served as precedents for the American experience, students will find a brief, well-illustrated discussion in *Europe: A Geographical Survey of the Continent* by Roy E. H. Mellor and E. Alistair Smith (New York: Columbia University Press, 1979). Another push and one will be almost back to the beginning. Then one is forced to come to terms with one of the grandest surveys of the urban experience in Western civilization. Lewis Mumford's *The City in History* (New York: Harcourt, Brace and World, 1961) is a magisterial study of "its origins, its transformations, and its prospects." Written from a deeply humanistic point of view, and from a certain polemical perspective, nearly every one of Mumford's 600 pages opens up a new way of looking at the city or of thinking about life. It is the type of book one could read as philosophy as well as history. It raises, at the very beginning, the most basic questions about what goes on in the streets, about public places, about a civic education, about what to do with life itself: "namely, whether [a person] should devote himself to the development of his own deepest humanity, or whether he shall surrender himself to the now almost automatic forces he himself has set in motion." The obedient creature of the second alternative, will, Mumford continues, have no need for the city, or, we might add, its streets or a guidebook to their interpretation.

·5·

Open Spaces

THE LAND IN ANY COMMUNITY CAN BE DIVIDED ROUGHLY
into three general categories: the streets, the individual lots or parcels that
have been improved with buildings, and a variety of open spaces, either
areas specifically designed for public use or parcels in an undeveloped state.
Our focus in this chapter is on the last of these categories—especially those
spaces used by people to meet each other in public; places where one can
expect to see other people and be seen by them. These places of encounter,
off the streets and out of doors, really have no word in the English language.
The best one can do is to list some of them: parks, playgrounds, vacant
lots, nature preserves, landings, cemeteries, parking lots, and scraps of land
seemingly left over after the community has been built.

Thus we might say there are two kinds of public open spaces: those for-
mally designated as such and set aside by the community to function as
open spaces and those areas used by various groups of people to serve the
same purpose, although not so designated by society. Examples of the first
type of open space usually show up on maps as parks, plazas, forest preserves,
and playgrounds. The second type of open space is much more difficult to
find in documents but is readily apparent to most people upon direct observation or personal reflection. These informal open spaces might best be considered first because they provide some insight into the public functions of
open spaces. In other words, one way to interpret the history of parks is
to start by observing the function of a vacant lot.

The Old Bog

One example from a suburb of Chicago dates from the early 1970s. Earlier developments in Glen Ellyn had placed rows of pleasant houses up and down the streets except for a tract of land that was poorly drained. To build on this land would not have been economical. Known to local people as "the peat bog," it became, in a subtle way, an integral part of the emerging community. Some years later, the pressure of the expanding metropolis made the old bog a prime spot to build new houses, even considering the added expense of excavation, drainage, and fill.

It was at this point that local residents, fearful of losing their open space, called in Alfred Etter, a naturalist from the Morton Arboretum. They hoped he would find some rare flower or exotic plants or animals on the tract. Perhaps if a rare orchid were there, a case could be made for preventing the transformation of the bog from informal open space to a site for attractive residences. It seems that open space was the real issue, not the concern for botanical rarities.

Etter's survey ("Argument for an Old Bog," in *The Morton Arboretum Quarterly* 10:1 [Spring 1974]: 1-8) reveals that the bog was "covered with nothing but the commonest of trees and weeds." As a trained observer of the landscape, however, the naturalist listed the ways in which the bog, now dried up in late summer, was used by the community:

•1. Transportation: The dry bog was crisscrossed with paths used as shortcuts by neighbors to get from one house to another.

•2. Health maintenance: Some of the people walking along the paths were going nowhere special but just getting exercise. Etter noted that space that could be used in this way was in short supply in the white-collar community.

•3. Aesthetic functions: The contrast of the vacant land with the houses surrounding it introduced a precious element of variety into the suburban neighborhood. It trained the eyes of the residents, Etter noted, so they could see the change of seasons and become familiar with the processes of birth, decay, and recycling—those important dimensions of life and our way of thinking about it.

•4. Landmark: The neighborhood merged imperceptibly into other suburban neighborhoods and needed some identifying feature to give it cohesion. The peat bog provided, in a way, a sense of belonging, "a bond of common experience," a community identity.

•5. Educational facility: Etter spent some time reflecting on how the vacant land gave children a space in which to dig caves, construct tree houses, and build an experiential base to give meaning to the textbooks in their schools. "Childhood," Etter observed, had in the electronic age, "become mostly 'show and tell' but little 'do.'" Here in the bog, the mind and body could learn together, and little children could crawl through the weeds on a "jungle adventure." The courage developed in these games, to face the unfamiliar, was an important goal of child development.

•6. Barometer for the quality of life: As a naturalist, Etter focused on the importance of the bog as a living encyclopedia or as a place to observe the natural processes at work. To the extent that the community functioned in harmony with Mother Earth, he implied, it uplifted the humanity of its citizens. The open space thus acted as a barometer to tell each person how the community was doing on the quality-of-life scale.

•7. Meeting place: Although Etter did not single out the use of the old bog as a meeting place, it was implied in several of the above functions. In the mind's eye, one can, no doubt, picture neighbors chatting while walking their dogs, or a new kid on the block being introduced to the rest of the gang at "the fort" hidden behind the tall weeds, or a teenage couple meeting at midpath "not really by chance."

Surely the list of uses for open spaces could be extended or refined, but even as it is, it will function well enough for our purpose. We want to understand the function of open spaces as public spaces. To help us put these areas into a historical perspective, of course, we need some documents. To challenge the list developed out of Etter's creative observations, let us use as our primary sources the old official reports of one park system.

Humboldt Park

A small bound volume contains the first annual reports of the West Chicago Park Commissioners for the years ending on February 28 or 29, 1870-1872 (fig. 5-1). What could these volumes tell us about the large regional park on Chicago's West Side that gave its name, Humboldt Park, to the community that surrounds it? Would Alfred Etter's observations on the old bog help us formulate questions to ask of these formal-looking documents? Would they help us as we strive to invest this piece of open space with meaning?

The first annual report began with a recitation of how the park district for this part of the city came into being. The legal entity was created by a state legislative act, which became law when signed by the governor on February 27, 1869. It was not until the end of April that the governor had selected the first members of the board, and they did not meet until

M. R. H. Warder

Lincoln Park

Compt. W. L. B. Jenney

FIRST

ANNUAL REPORT

OF

WEST CHICAGO

PARK COMMISSIONERS,

For the Year ending

FEBRUARY 28, 1870.

W. LB. JENNEY,
520 NEW YORK LIFE BLDG.,
CHICAGO.

CHICAGO :

W. CRAVENS & CO., BOOK AND JOB PRINTERS,

144 South Water Street.

Fig. 5-1. First Annual Report of West Chicago Park Commissioners for the Year ending February 28, 1870. The formal annual reports issued by governmental agencies and other institutions often provide much essential information and record the materials in chronological order. Note that this copy belonged to the landscape architect and was inscribed by him. Jenney later became a noted architect and is remembered today as "the father of the skyscraper."

May 5. As a local government agency, the park board was given specific boundaries and powers, including those of taxation up to a certain limit. In addition, the law specified that there were to be at least three parks in the district, each to be at least a certain size and to be developed from land purchased for less than a specified amount, and that these parks were to be connected by a boulevard extending to the boundaries of the district where it would connect with similar parkways to be built by the North (Lincoln) and the South Chicago Park Commissioners (fig. 5-2).

Thus the legislature, in creating this agency of local government, carefully spelled out how the parks were to fit into the general plan of the metropolis. The law furnishes another example of how the city plan shapes the individual parts of a community. The power of the board, however, was "so prescribed by limitations and restrictions" that it went through a dozen plans before one was found that was both in conformity to the law and acceptable to the public.

The first annual report recites a litany of problems faced by the commissioners as they sought to do their work. Once the site of the parks had been determined, the value of land in the vicinity rapidly increased, and people who owned the lands designated for parkland naturally held out for more money. Some taxpayers challenged the legality of the park commission by bringing suits in both the state and federal courts. Another problem was to secure proper drainage to make the parklands usable throughout the year. This often involved getting the cooperation and assistance of neighboring landowners.

In spite of the problems, the president of the board concluded his part of the report on an encouraging note. The financial reports, which followed, presented interesting examples of how the public funds were spent. The first expenditure went for certified copies of the legislative act, so that each commissioner would know the responsibilities and restrictions resting on the board. The second expenditure was for a large map of the city. Others followed for a seal, stationery, advertising, office fixtures, and even an awning and some window screens. A table at the conclusion of the document summarized the work of the board during the first year. The names for the parks and boulevards had already been selected and were used in the chart. Humboldt Park was to be at least 200 acres, and the board had already acquired by purchase or donation almost 75 acres of this land.

The second annual report is a longer document. The president's report was largely devoted to suggesting ways the original legislation might be

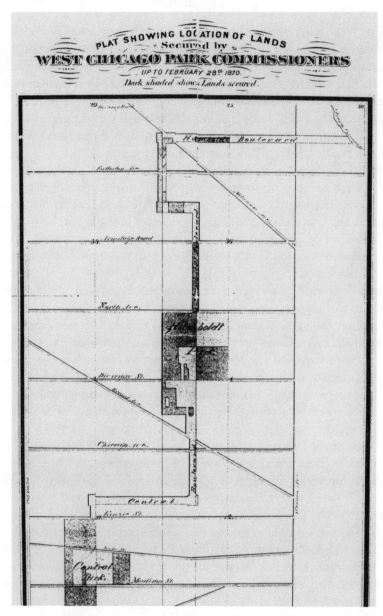

Fig. 5-2. Plat Showing Location of Lands Secured by West Chicago Park Commissioners up to February 28th, 1870. This map, which accompanied the first annual report, clearly shows how the future parks were to be connected by parkways. The progress of land acquisition is indicated by the shaded areas within the boundaries of the future parks.

amended, so that the purposes of the parks might be more fully realized. The major issue was to increase the tax revenue in order to improve and purchase the parklands. "No great public work can be carried forward," George W. Stanford declared, "without a liberal outlay of money, and the only way of raising this money is by taxation" (p. 7). The president then cited other cities' experiences that showed that the value of lands near parks increased substantially more than the taxes paid by the owners to purchase the park site and to develop it. "As a general thing, taxes are paid for an article, or improvement, which ministers to the necessities or convenience of the people, and add very largely in excess of their cost to the general wealth" (p. 8). The lots immediately adjacent to the new parks, even in an undeveloped state, had increased in value by three, four, or even five times.

Open space, in other words, added to the value of the lots nearby. Improving the open space by creating parks would keep the land values increasing. The benefits would be reaped not only by individual owners but by the entire community as well. "It is a notorious fact," Stanford continued, that Chicago "with all its business and commercial advantages" lacked property of "sufficient attraction" to house those who had accumulated "well-earned fortunes. This class of men, while still clinging to Chicago for business advantages, have sought homes in neighboring towns and cities, upon which they have lavished large sums of money." Thousands of suburban families would have built homes in the city "but for want of the very pleasures the parks are designed to furnish."

All of a sudden the dull annual report springs to life. The reader is tempted to read the prose out loud, in the style of a nineteenth-century orator: "The appropriation asked for by the board would enable us to transform this open prairie from its present level surface into hills and lakes, with shaded drives and walks. . . . trees and shrubbery will entirely change the face of the parks, and make them at once, places of beauty and of pleasant resort. . . . [The parks] will, from year to year, become more and more a source of gratification to that just pride which animates a good citizen" (p. 13).

The second annual report concluded with a message from the firm of Jenney, Schermerhorn and Bogart, architects and engineers for the project, who began with some helpful comments on the nature and purpose of the parks. First, the West Chicago parks were to be part of a city-wide system of large parks and connecting ways, which would make them accessible from all parts of the city. These parks were to be created from undeveloped land beyond the built-up region, but directly in "the line of free city extension." When development would come to the area, the firm predicted, the commissioners would receive a double measure of praise. "They will have made the city attractive" by providing "elegance and refinement of recreation which experience has shown determines the permanent residence of many whose means give them opportunity for free choice." In addition, the mass of people would also benefit from the raised standards of public health and the opportunity to use the parks.

Thus the development of these open spaces served three general purposes: to define an attractive city plan, to be magnets for upper- and middle-class housing, and to promote public health and recreation. The problems that faced the landscape architects in building parks that would realize these goals are worth repeating because they help us comprehend the nature of the final designs (fig. 5-3). The sites in 1870 were flat, poorly drained prairie lands, "without appreciable undulation of surface or a single specimen of forest growth worth preserving." Moreover, the parks lay beyond the built-up portion of the city whose existing drainage system was not designed to reach out to these lands. The park district would need to construct its own sewers, a fact that explains the manhole covers on Chicago's boulevards marked with the park district's name or initials. To save expense, the park drainage system could be much smaller in size if reservoirs could be built in the parks to store some of the run off for discharge at a slower rate over a period of days or weeks. The excavation of these lakes would then provide dirt for the building of small hills and for creating that variety of topography the architects thought was missing. Necessity became the mother of invention.

But the parks in the rough, the report concluded, would not be very appealing to the taxpayers. "They cannot be expected to imagine what the park is eventually to be, from unsightly piles of topsoil or the rough work of the gradings." Therefore, it was "highly desirable to exhibit, at the earliest practicable moment, at least a portion of finished ground; that will be a bright spot amid dull surroundings, attractive to the visitor, and a foretaste of what they may expect in the future" (p. 81).

The president's section in the *Third Annual Report. . . for the Year Ending February 29th, 1872* was much shorter than normal, limited to a few details on the board's plan for securing the necessary revenues to put the park system into functioning order. The list of expenditures, however, provided many hints about the progress being made. Items like shrubs, sprinkling carts, road rollers, and bills for mowing grass or hauling manure suggest that the land-

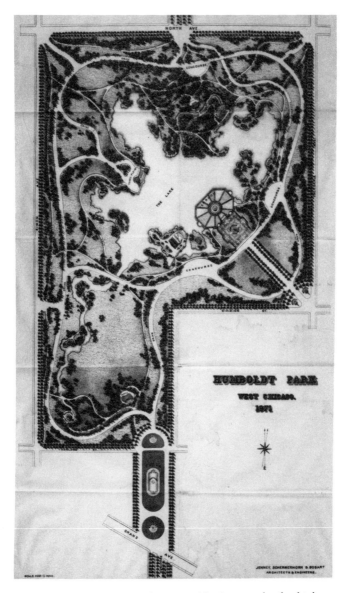

Fig. 5-3. Humboldt Park, Chicago, 1871. The proposed landscaping plan for this large park focused on the lake. The creation of this body of water had several distinct advantages. The earth removed from the site to create the lake bed could be used to transform the flat prairie into a series of rolling hills. Moreover, the lake itself would significantly reduce the need for expensive drainage facilities to make the park usable in wet weather. Finally, the lake enhanced the visitor's perception of nature and his or her sense of escape for the city.

Fig. 5-4. The proposed Chicago Fire Monument, to be erected in the city's Central Park on the West Side, was a fascinating idea. The shaft was to be composed of the safes that survived the fire. Similarly, the decorative stone work of the base was to use items salvaged from the ruins. The materials were brought to the site (see figure 5-5), but the edifice was apparently never erected.

scaping had moved to the final stages, in at least the "demonstration section" of the park. A curious item, however, appeared toward the end of the year 1871: "hauling relics for fire monument."

The report from the architect and engineer, also uncharacteristically brief, offered a terse explanation. "The work proceeded rapidly and without interruption until the fire of October 8th." The Chicago Fire had cut short the year's work. Shortly after the ashes had cooled, the architect was instructed to design a fire monument "to be constructed of safes and other relics, obtainable from the ruins" (fig. 5-4). Stone from the ruined buildings was to be used for the base of the structure, "surmounted by a tall pyramid, formed of iron safes, and terminated by a tall iron column supporting a globe of cast iron." A series of eight columns would then form a ring around the base of the monument. A total of 219 relic safes, plus the needed columns and stone, had been brought to the Central Park (fig. 5-5), but the fire monument was never completed. The parks themselves proved to be a more fitting memorial to the people who erected a new city out of the ashes of the old.

In looking to the coming season of work, William LeBaron Jenney, the

Fig. 5-5. "View in Central Park, showing Relics for 'Fire Monument'" is a photograph posted in an addendum to some copies of the third annual report of the park commissioners in 1872. Looking at the assortment of salvaged material, one can get a fairly good idea about why the monument was never erected.

architect and engineer urged that efforts be concentrated on completing the "demonstration" portion of the park, especially "in case the contemplated expenditure is limited." The finished portion could be be used at times by the public, and it could serve as a stimulus to complete the task. "The drives and walks would have earth surfaces, it is true, but with a little care, these could be kept in good condition, if used only in dry weather" (p. 39).

As if to spur the commissioners to greater efforts, Jenney included with his report a series of "photographic views," some of which were pasted into the copies of the document. One showed the drab and monotonous view before work commenced (fig. 5-6); the other traced the progress of the work to date (fig. 5-7).

The real prizes in the report, as we look at it today, are the engraved plans for the various parks, each one dominated by a small lake (fig. 5-3). A knowledge of the engineering problems that Jenney faced puts the lagoons in a new perspective. They were not only centerpieces for the landscaping; they were also the fundamental device for transforming the vacant prairie into usable parkland. They stood for utility and efficiency as well as beauty and ornament. As the key improvement in the landscape, they were instrumental in transforming an informal open space into a formal one.

Etter's old bog was soon filled with houses, but Humboldt Park continues today as a major regional park among the teeming neighborhoods of Chicago's West Side. We could follow the development of this open space by continuing our survey of the annual reports and richly supplement them with maps, post cards, real estate promotional tracts, dedication speeches, and a variety of other documents. But we have gone far enough into the narrative, and it is time to put the naturalist's observations about open space and the story of Humboldt Park's origins together into a general discussion on the interpretation of public or open spaces.

Interpreting Open Spaces

Transportation. Alfred Etter's first observation about the use of the old bog was to point out its function as an aid to transportation. It is interesting to note how this same point proved to be of paramount importance in the establishment of the West Chicago Park System. The law establishing the parks required a series of parkways or boulevards that were to connect all of the city's major parks and extend the benefits of this "chain of verdure" to residents in every neighborhood. Cartographers soon used the system of

Fig. 5-6. "View of the Park Lands in 1870" was another photograph pasted in the annual report. It documents very well the limitations of the site for a picturesque park. The contrast between this view and the splendid drawing in figure 5-3 shows how much the Victorian concept of nature was a product of cultural forces.

Fig. 5-7. This "View in Humboldt Park Showing Lake Excavation in Spring, 1872" should be compared with the site pictured in figure 5-6. It shows the first modest steps taken in the transformation of the prairie lands into a picturesque landscape. Some of the newly planted trees seem to be elms.

parks and parkways as basic reference points when designing street maps and public transportation guides for the city. The boulevard system, from which all trucks were later excluded, retained its dual function as a park and a pleasure drive for at least three generations of urban dwellers. The parks and boulevards formed the backbone of Chicago's system of bikeways developed during the energy crisis of the 1970s. In 1986, several students of the city were urging that the system be made to function once more. Anyone who is trying to understand a park or an open space would do well to relate it first to the basic transportation patterns in the community.

Health. The large parks created for the industrial cities in nineteenth-century America were often referred to as the "lungs of the metropolis." But very few of these parks were carved out of crowded tenement districts. Most, like Humboldt Park in Chicago, Central Park in New York, or Golden Gate Park in San Francisco, were designed for the outer fringes of the city. Only later did the built-up areas expand to surround the parkland with residential neighborhoods. The relationship between the parks, or open space, and public health, must, therefore, be sought on grounds that merely supplement the usual appeals for admitting sunshine and fresh air into crowded city streets.

Many of the early arguments for public parks stressed the psychological need of urban dwellers to be in contact with nature. A laborer working on Chicago's West Side parks in the 1870s said that "every person, to be happy, must occasionally see a tree, and he must be able to look over a stretch of water." Dr. John R. Rauch, one of the most vocal advocates of parks in Chicago at the time of the 1869 legislation, published in that year a long pamphlet on *Public Parks: Their Effects upon the Moral, Physical, and Sanitary Condition of the Inhabitants of Large Cities.* He thought that there was a direct relationship between vegetation, especially trees, and public health. As urban structures displaced the natural vegetation, the climate degenerated and diseases took hold. His study contains page after page of tables relating wind direction to mortality and suggesting that the proper planting of trees in parks could modify the ill effects of unhealthful winds. Parks, or open spaces, in other words, directly influenced a family's health even if they never set foot on its paths or picnicked in its groves.

An important way cities promoted the health of their citizenry was by providing appropriate places for physical exercise and wholesome recreation.

Etter's remarks on the value of the old bog as a place for active pursuits repeated a refrain about parks being "not merely breathing-and-beauty-spots but [they] are truly the playgrounds of the people, who are permitted to spread out for games. . . in every direction" (Alfred Granger, *Chicago Welcomes You* [Chicago: A. Kroch, 1933], p. 165). However, the early documents of the public parks movement make it clear that the relationship between open spaces in the city and the health of its citizens should be constructed in much broader terms, a point that logically leads to a consideration of the aesthetic function of open spaces.

Aesthetics. To the Victorian mind, truth and beauty, citizenship and morality, were all interconnected, and they could be encouraged, in concert, by regular contact with the beauties of nature. Using the English-style of landscaping, Humboldt Park and most of the other parks created in nineteenth-century America tried to imitate the best views that nature could provide: a gently rolling terrain with a variety of land forms, a mixture of vegetation types where clusters of trees and shrubs set off broad grassy areas, and an interplay between land and water afforded by mirror-like lagoons, picturesque bridges, and sparkling fountains.

Note how the landscape architect for the West Chicago parks thought that the flat, open prairie was ill-suited for parks. It had no variety, no picturesque qualities, and only limited possibilities for aesthetic expression. In the 1980s, however, many friends of the parks and advocates for open lands wished that some of the natural landscape had been preserved in the metropolitan area. The modern appeal for ecological understanding came out of a different context. To Jenney and his contemporaries, the very definition of a park called for certain enhancements by human creativity. A park without statues, monuments, fountains, buildings, flower beds, and exotic plans was almost unthinkable.

Andrew Jackson Downing, the foremost of the early advocates for public parks, writing in 1848, assumed that a bandstand would be a part of every public park. The aesthetic dimension of the public place thus went beyond the visual aspect of the landscape, the buildings, the gardens, and the monuments. Parks were supposed to create different auditory environments as well: a quiet place to escape the din of city business, a retreat to hear the "song of the lark" and other voices of nature, and a concert grove "where the best music could be heard daily."

Landmarks. In his celebrated "Talk about Public Parks and Gardens" (1848), Downing referred to the popularity of the new, romantically landscaped cemeteries as models for public parks. The only difference, he noted, would be the omission of monuments. His advice, though, was never seriously considered. The new parks were quickly furnished with a variety of civic monuments such as statues, fountains, and historical memorabilia. One of the earliest monuments proposed for Central Park in New York was a bust of Downing himself, a work that was to be accompanied by a long inscription. The national crisis of 1860 delayed the memorial, but in the aftermath of the Civil War, the country soon enjoyed a climate for the erection of statues and commemorative sculptures throughout the land.

The desire to furnish the parks and public places with landmarks can be seen in the plans for the West Chicago parks. The ashes had hardly cooled from the Chicago Fire when the park commissioners requested that Jenney design an appropriate monument to the catastrophic event. Someone had the idea of using actual relics from the ruins as the materials for the shrine, and considerable funds were expended to haul foundation stones, columns, and safes to the site.

Other features in the parks could also serve as landmarks: buildings, lagoons, floral displays, fountains, bridges, and animals in cages. One Chicago park housed a very large bear in a den, another had a tethered eagle, and a third received some swans from the Public Garden in Boston. These animals became attractions, and their locations provided important "fix points" on the mental maps residents carried around in their heads.

Etter noted how the very presence of the old bog gave the Glen Ellyn neighborhood a sense of identity and served as a central landmark. This was true for the West Chicago parks as well. To this day, the residential areas nearby use the park names to designate the communities. An advertisement for the Humboldt Park subdivision of S. E. Gross, a noted developer of working-class housing in Chicago, shows how the parks helped to define an urban community in 1891 (fig. 5-8). The advertisement itself uses the main entrance to Humboldt Park as point of reference for prospective buyers. Glancing at the map in the advertisement to search for landmarks, one can see how the lake, a floral display, or a gazebo could function as a reference point for the new development.

Education. Etter's emphasis on how children could learn by doing in the old bog contrasts rather sharply with the idea of open space in nineteenth-

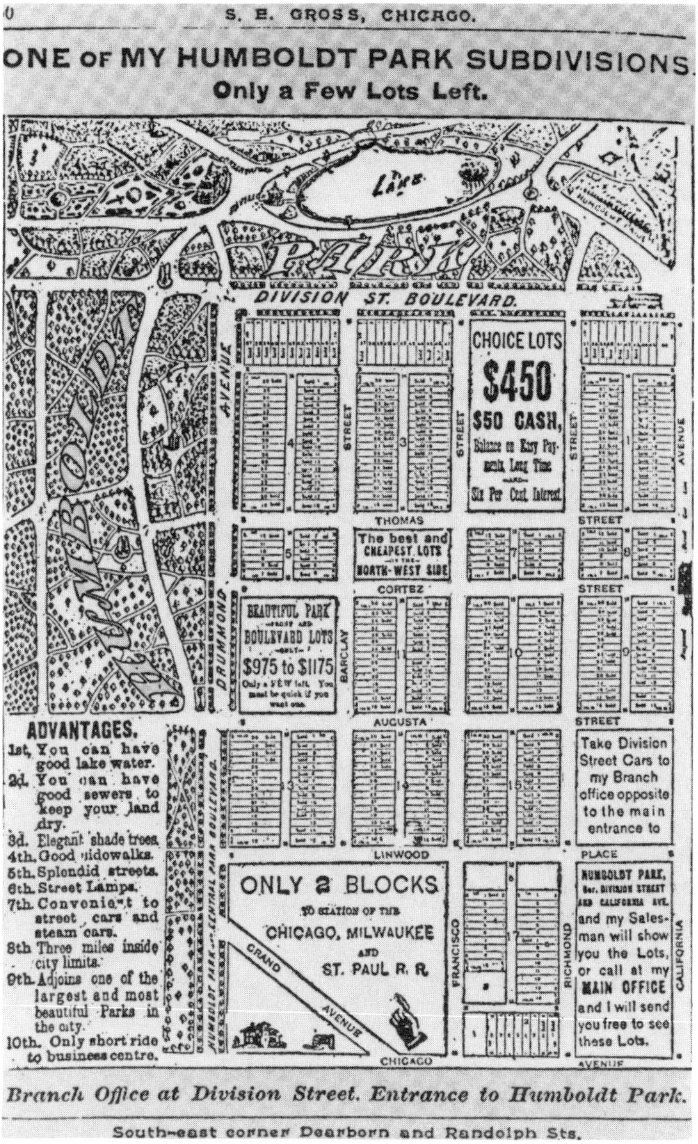

Fig. 5-8. This subdivision adjacent to Humboldt Park was laid out after the park was under construction. Some lots were still available at a modest price when this real estate catalogue was issued. The "cottages" built on the less expensive lots housed working-class families. A house and a lot could be purchased for about $2.500. The lots next to the park, the "boulevard lots," were twice as expensive. To create more of these higher priced lots, the orientation of the lots along Division Street shifted to a north-south direction.

century America. Jenney's plans for the parks do not incorporate any special areas for children to play. Even for adults, the parks emphasized facilities for passive recreation. To be sure, the founders of American parks thought of them as educational facilities, but their reasoning moved more in the direction of appreciative looking, listening, and reflecting than active involvement in physical exercise or hands-on educational experiences.

One of the major interpretive themes for the history of any park established before 1900 is to note how it changed over the years from a passive spectator-type facility to one that provided the means for active participation. At the beginning, it seems that planners expected the typical visitors to a park to be family units, and the planners emphasized things that would appeal to adults of the upper-middle class. Gradually the parks were adapted for use by a variety of ages, economic classes, and ethnic groups. In every case, as park facilities became more diverse, they also moved in the direction of more active participation by the visitors.

The park movement was clearly part of a broad movement for popular refinement and the development in each individual citizen of his or her highest potential. "It takes up popular education," Downing noted 1851, "where the common school and ballot box leave it and raises the working man to the same level of enjoyment with the man of leisure and accomplishment."

Barometers. Imagine a conversation, on a park bench, of course, between William LeBaron Jenney, the landscape architect; John Rauch, the advocate of parks from a public health perspective; and Alfred Etter, the naturalist. Each person would, no doubt, comment on the vista before him in a different way, but all would probably agree that the scene could serve as a barometer to measure the quality of life in the community. As the conversation developed, an observer could list the points on which the three were in essential agreement:

1. Human beings need contact with the natural environment in order to be healthy in a physical, emotional, and spiritual sense.

2. The development of industrial cities has largely destroyed the natural environment, to the detriment of the populace.

3. It is the mission of public parks to bring back to the cities the benefits of nature and to provide each citizen with the opportunity to walk through a natural landscape.

4. The extent to which a city provides these opportunities and the extent to

which it develops open spaces to serve the needs of its citizens are ways to measure the progress of democracy.

The idea of progress clearly underlays the arguments for public parks from
the 1850s onward. The city of tomorrow would be better than the city of
yesterday as the present generation built parks and developed their potential. The presence of ruins in the landscape, like those relics from the Chicago
Fire, was an appropriate way to make the parks calendars of civic progress.
In this sense, parks were more than just barometers of public responsibility;
they served as clocks as well, recording the civic time and registering the
progress make from generation to generation.

Meeting places. Parks were thus places where the past could meet the present. In a more obvious sense, they were spots where families and friends
could meet, where people of similar interests in art or music or sports could
join together. It was even more important that people of different neighborhoods, economic classes, social status, and ethnic backgrounds could come
together and participate in the same activities in these public places. Frederick
Law Olmsted thought that Central Park in New York most fully met the
city's need for a public meeting place when 50,000 people came to ice skate
on a wintry Sunday afternoon.

It was not so much that people from different stations and backgrounds
would get to know one another as individuals; rather the parks were to provide shared moments of exhilaration in the out-of-doors, a common sense
of place, and enjoyment of the same beauties of nature. These were essential building blocks out of which democratic loyalties and patriotic aspirations could be built. Currier and Ives, ever alert to images that would capture
the spirit of the day, produced a popular picture of the ice skating in Central Park in 1862. In the midst of the Civil War, it seemed to testify to the
solidarity of the commonwealth and to predict an optimistic future.

But there was another way, more melancholy in tone, in which parks served
as meeting places. The vegetation, as it marked the changes in seasons, also
reminded the observer of the passage of the years and the course of a life
time. Here one met the prospect of death itself. This was a personal time
scale rather than a natural or a civic one. It led, not to another round in
the cycle or to a progressively better city in the future, but to immortality
itself. Perhaps tombstones would not be so out of place in a park after all.

The role of parks as places where individuals met their destiny was stated
rather dramatically by Frederika Bremer, paraphrasing a letter she had writ-

ten to Downing from Cuba about 1850. She had just meditated on the lush subtropical vegetation, and the experience set off a train of reflections on her friend's vocation in the hereafter. The Creator, she was convinced, would reserve a star for Downing to embellish with his horticultural designs. "You will build a cathedral," she wrote, "where every plant and every creature will be as a link rising upwards, joining in one harmonious Apocalypse revealing the glory of the Creator" (in Andrew Jackson Downing, *Rural Essays*, ed. by George William Curtis [New York: R. Worthington, 1881], p. lxx). The park on earth was also a cathedral, a place for worshipers to meet the Almighty, thus fulfilling its highest function and meeting its most sublime purpose.

Suggested Readings

As is the case with so much history, the best and most stimulating works are primary sources themselves. All histories of public parks in the United States begin with the suggestive essays by Andrew Jackson Downing in the *Horticulturist*, a journal he edited between 1846 and 1852. These were later collected and edited by George William Curtis (New York: R. Worthington, 1881). The key articles are "A Talk about Public Parks and Gardens" (October 1848), "The New York Park" (August 1851), and "Public Cemeteries and Public Gardens" (July 1849).

Of even greater interest is the account on *Creating Central Park, 1857-1861*, which forms volume 3 of the *Papers of Frederick Law Olmsted* (Baltimore: The Johns Hopkins University Press, 1983). This volume, edited by Charles E. Beveridge and David Schuyler, has a splendid introduction, a wide-ranging collection of documents on the origin of America's most celebrated park, copious notes, and an eighty-page pictorial essay that includes maps and diagrams. A student looking for interpretive themes and research topics will be richly rewarded by paging through this fine study. It is impressive to see how many themes of the later park movement were announced in the building of the prototype park.

Albert Fein's brief study of *Frederick Law Olmsted and the American Environmental Tradition* (New York: George Braziller, 1972) will help place the Central Park experience into several broader contexts. First, it shows how the park expressed the utopian ideals of the American democratic tradition. Second, it traces the interaction of these principles with the social and political realities of life in the big city. A section of Fein's study on Central Park is titled "A Major Defeat: Parks and Politics." The third virtue of Fein's book is that it prints more than a hundred photographs, maps, plans, and diagrams covering all aspects of Olmsted's career, from parks and colleges campuses to suburbs and urban neighborhoods.

FLO: A Biography of Frederick Law Olmsted by Laura Wood Roper (Baltimore: The Johns Hopkins University Press, 1973) is the standard biography, written directly out of the subject's papers. There are three chapters on the origins of Central Park, but some of the later chapters on "New Parks, New Suburbs, 1868-1872" and "Shaping a Profession" should not be overlooked.

A brief appreciation of Olmsted as an artist and Central Park as his masterpiece is in *American Space: The Centennial Years, 1865-1876* by John Brinckerhoff Jackson (New York: Norton, 1972). This suggestive study, which discusses the development of open spaces in several cities, calls particular attention to the work of H. W. S. Cleveland who took up the task of developing the South Chicago parks after the fire of 1871 destroyed most of the plans originally proposed by the firm of Olmsted and Vaux. Cleveland's work in Chicago and elsewhere, as well as his writing, soon made him an important influence in the landscaping of parks. His *Landscape Architecture as Applied to the Wants of the West*, originally published in 1873, has been reprinted in a modern edition, edited by Roy Lubove (Pittsburgh: The University of Pittsburgh Press, 1965).

A brief, general treatment of "the origins of Chicago's park system, 1850-1875" is Glen E. Holt's "Private Plans for Public Spaces," *Chicago History* 8:3 (Fall 1979): 173-184. The journals of state and local historical societies are always good places to look for materials on the development of parks in a particular locality. One fine example for Chicago is Michael P. McCarthy's "Politics and the Parks: Chicago Businessmen and the Recreation Movement," *Journal of the Illinois State Historical Society* 65:2 (Summer 1972): 158-172, which documents how the support of business interests was crucial to the success of the early parks.

Other helpful sources on the origins of parks are the large local histories produced in the late nineteenth century, often by firms specializing in the business. The foremost example of this type of book dealing with Humboldt Park is the third volume of the *History of Chicago* by Alfred T. Andreas (Chicago: A. T. Andreas Company, 1886). It devotes a whole chapter to the parks and boulevards. Numerous illustrations and statistics supplement the text. A helpful feature supplied by Andreas is a series of biographies of eight individuals prominent in the promotion of Chicago's parks. All of them, it turns out, had extensive interests in real estate.

To place the later development of parks into an interpretive framework, one will want to sample the periodical literature listed in the *Readers' Guide*. A good summary of the types of parks and their use is chapter 12 in *The Urban Environment* by Samuel E. Wallace (Homewood, Ill.: The Dorsey Press, 1980). Wallace uses New York City as an example and rightly praises the study on parks in the *Regional Survey of New York and Its Environs* (8 Volumes, 1927-1929). This volume, *Public Recreation: A Study of Parks, Playgrounds, and Other Outdoor Recreation Facilities* (New York: Regional Plan of New York, 1928) by Lee F. Hamner is full of detailed observations, statistical reports, maps, charts, and informed commentaries.

More recent discussion on open spaces in the American city can be found in *Parks for People* by Ben Whitaker and Kenneth Browns (New York: Schocken Books, 1971) and *Open Spaces: The Life of American Cities* by August Herkscher (Twentieth Century Fund Essay, New York: Harper and Row, 1977). The latter study, based on an extensive tour of America's parks and interviews with park officials, emphasizes how urban open spaces are "associated with pleasure, with recreation, with human encounters and communal celebrations." Herkscher envisioned open space as the key to renewing and stablilizing urban life. His study may be considered the culmination of a movement to make the public aware of the importance of public spaces in the modern city, a drive that began, perhaps, with William H. Whyte's polemical book on *The Last Landscape* (Garden City, N.Y.: Doubleday, 1968).

Every student will also want to consult Galen Granz, *The Politics of Park Design: A History of Urban Parks in America* (Cambridge, Mass.: MIT Press, 1983), one of the most recent and best documented scholarly studies. The book combines insights from architecture, political science, sociology, and history. On the sociology of particular neighborhood parks, one of the most influential studies is Gerald D. Suttles, *The Social Order of the Slum: Ethnicity and Territory in the Inner City* (Chicago: University of Chicago Press, 1968). Some of its useful features are maps showing how the parks were carved up into territories for use by particular groups defined by age, sex, and ethnic origin. Suttles also shows how the parks were part of a network of public spaces that had carefully defined functions and populations at any given time of the day. After reading Suttles, one will be impressed with the necessity for careful field observation to understand fully the function of urban open spaces. The documents will take you only so far.

Urban Space: A Brief History of the City Square by Jere Stuart French (Dubuque, Iowa: Kendall/Hunt, 1983) is something like a textbook for students of city planning and urban design. It emphasizes the tradition of civic open space in Western civilization, often making its points with excellent sketches, drawings, and photographs. Chapter 8, "Order Diversified: The City Park," goes too far in contrasting parks and city squares, but beginning students will find a lot of useful ideas in this profusely illustrated book.

Barrie B. Greenbie's *Spaces: Dimensions of the Human Landscape* (New Haven: Yale University Press, 1981) conveys its message through both text and pictures. Its chapter on "Humane Space: Promenades, Parks, and Places for Peace of Mind" uses a somewhat technical vocabulary, but it also asks major questions and concludes that one needs to visit both urban public spaces, such as Central Park, and quiet, natural landscapes, such as the old bog or a national park, to "feel fully at one with the human race" (p. 220).

·6·

Public Places in a Community

HOW CAN INSIGHTS INTO THE NATURE AND HISTORY OF public places, deepen an understanding of a community? How can we use the suggestions in the previous chapters to sharpen our appreciation for the places where we live and the ones we will visit? How can we put together the comments about monuments, buildings, plans, streets, and open spaces?

History is, after all, concerned with change. Without change there can be no history. A big advantage of nearby history is that one usually starts with a fairly good understanding of the present, and this knowledge helps us measure the change from the past to the present. Therefore, a good place to start a project on nearby history, it seems to me, is with some up-to-date maps or plans of the community. For large towns and cities, maps and plans often present a confusing amount of detail or are so large that it is desirable to have at hand a generalized, smaller-scale map. In addition, we might need a large-scale map for the central business district or the historical core of the community in order to identify specific buildings and landmarks.

The challenge is to take these maps apart mentally, to search for evidence about how the community developed over time. Old maps will be a great help, since one can readily compare them to contemporary maps. Eventually one would like to line up, decade by decade, a sequence of town plans from the founding of the community, up to the present. As the story of the community unfolds in this historical atlas, it almost by definition focuses on public places. As a map of one decade merges into the next, public places, such as streets, squares, monuments, parks, and landmark buildings, provide the points of reference and the indexes of change. The geographic setting, it is true, also provides a frame of reference for comparing one map with the next. Rivers, lakes, harbors, hills, and valleys always set the basic

97

outlines for a community plan, but they do not often provide hints about the social dynamics, the economic transactions, and the cultural transmissions taking place at the site. On the other hand, public places have the potential to illustrate these themes. That is why monuments, buildings, parks, and the like offer such useful tools to help us understand the maps before us and the communities they portray.

The purpose of this chapter is to help make such maps of a community come alive by noting how public places animate the cartographic records. Then, as we travel through the cityscape we can draw upon the interpretive resources in our mental bank. Our feeling for the impact of time will make us sensitive to the processes of change. But to measure the nature and extent of change, we need some markers to insert into the community's chronology. These mileposts will divide the past into readily understood segments, or eras, and will help us sort the historical forces at work. Every community needs a few turning points or watershed events to divide its history into periods. A number of periodization schemes could be used (see Appendix A), but the idea of the "three cities," which we are about to discusss, is the most useful concept for us to have as we read our maps, take our walks, and do our research.

The Concept of "Three Cities"

The idea of "three cities" is based on the observation that American communities have gone through three general phases of development. Each phase is based on the primary means of transportation its citizens used to get around the town. Thus the history of a typical city has three periods: the walking city, the streetcar city, and the automobile city. The tripartite scheme affords a simple and convincing way to characterize the development of public places.

There are several essential questions to ask about the beginning of each community's development: How did the first residents get here? What means of transportation did they use? When the founders laid out the town, how did they expect people would arrive and depart? How did they expect residents to get from one part of town to another? Was the original settlement oriented to a harbor or a lake, a river or a canal, a highway or a railroad? As we look at the maps in front of us with these questions in mind, we need to locate the original area of settlement. Where is the historical core of the community?

Chances are the town began with some sort of public place as a nucleus.

Perhaps it was a trading post, a fort, a crossroads, or a seat of government. Around this central place of meeting, a town gradually emerged, and it developed a system of internal transportation to supplement the original roads and trails. Some communities, of course, never developed enough to extend beyond the original street or crossroads. They remain today as one- or two-street hamlets, places where motorists slow down as they pass through but joke about not blinking for fear they will miss the community. Here the major public place is the road itself.

If the community grew enough in the early period to develop a system of side streets and byways, it probably assumed many of the characteristics of the walking city. Since most people traveled around the town on foot, the various urban functions were mixed up and placed close by each other. People found it convenient to live and work, to shop and worship, to seek entertainment and education all in the same neighborhood. Few walking cities developed specialized districts; instead almost every block served a variety of needs. A building might house a store in front, a workshop in back, and residences above, with a church next door and a stable on the side. Residents could spend entire weeks or months without venturing more than a few blocks from home. One specialized area, the warehouse district, was closely tied to transportation facilities. Another was the mill district, depending on a source of power and usually located along a stream below some rapids.

The size of the walking city was, in some ways, limited by how far it was convenient to walk from the edge of town to the core of urban services at the center. A radius of two miles usually marked the fullest extent of cities at this stage of development. Since residents could easily get from their own homes to other points in the city, maps of the community were needed only by visitors.

If a community grew beyond a certain population, there was pressure to extend upward and to use every possible space within the built-up area. As buildings crowded together, open spaces tended to disappear. Yards were filled with additional houses, sheds, and stockpiles of goods. It became a symbol of wealth and status to have a garden or open space around one's residence and yet to live in close proximity to the urban core. Mansions and social clubs for the wealthy in the heart of town, dating back to the walking city era, still exist in many communities.

Rails changed the city and ushered in a new period of development. The tracks extended the urban area in two ways. First, the scheduling of daily passenger service by the new railroads led to the development of residential suburbs in favored locations out of town. Families with enough means could build homes beyond the congestion and noise of the city and then commute to a place of work on "accommodation cars," which were attached to the milk trains. In time, commuter runs and local passenger trains became regular services in larger metropolitan areas.

The transformation of the city for most residents came from the second vehicle to use the rails, the streetcar. Streetcar suburbs were built immediately adjacent to the old walking city. At first, between 1830 and 1870, when horse-drawn omnibuses were placed on tracks for short runs, the cars were small and could hold only a few passengers. The lines were used mainly to connect public buildings, such as train stations, hotels, and government buildings. With the extension of the tracks, however, it became possible for people living at the end of the line to reach the center of the city at a reasonable cost. Additional housing sprang up along these routes, and urban sprawl got its start.

Inventors tried to develop more powerful and more efficient means of locomotion for the streetcars, at first using small steam locomotives, called "dummies," to replace horses. In 1873, Andrew S. Halldie developed a moving cable for locomotion in San Francisco. Other cities soon followed the example and set up extensive cable-car systems powered by large, steam-driven machinery at powerhouses near the midpoint of the lines. Moving cables extended under the streets, and the cars gripped onto the cables for their power. At the end of the line, the cable turned around in a loop to go in the other direction, a term which probably explains the name of Chicago's central business district, "the Loop."

The use of electric motors on each streetcar proved to be a major breakthrough in the 1880s. At first the current to run the motors was transmitted by the tracks, but the electrical hazard in the public way, as well as the danger of short circuits in wet weather, caused most systems to switch to trolley wires. Frank J. Sprague solved most of the problems of trolleys when he designed a streetcar system for Richmond, Virginia, in 1888.

The horse-drawn streetcars and cable systems had pushed the radius of the city's built-up area out to three or four miles. With trolleys, the limits of the city could extend eight or ten miles from the center. The streetcar developments then overlapped with the railroad suburbs, providing alternative means of mass transportation in some areas. Just before the turn of the century, the introduction of electric interurban trains and elevated tracks further bound the metropolitan regions together in a network of rails.

A glance at the map of Chicago (fig. 6-1), perhaps the prototype nineteenth-century American city, shows how the system of large parks described in chapter 5 marked the transition area between the horse-car zone and the trolley neighborhoods. When the parks were designed about 1870, it was

Fig. 6-1. Map of Chicago Showing the Wards, Streets, and Parks. The map shows a major city after its first decade as a streetcar city. Development has not yet completely surrounded the parks to the west of the city. Railroads for horse-drawn vehicles and trains are indicated on the map. The shaded area shows the extent of the Chicago Fire of 1871. It marks the approximate extent of the old walking city. (Chicago: Rufus Blanchard, 1870s).

assumed that people would reach the greenery at the edge of the city by horse-drawn vehicles or on foot. Note how the parks were spread around the city, placing them within the two-mile walking limit for the bulk of the population.

As development pushed beyond the parks into the neighborhoods served by trolley streetcars, the houses were gradually set farther back on their lots, creating more "common space" between the street and house facade. These front yards served as a transitional space between the street and the private quarters of the home. The land was privately owned but served a public function. It reflected a "freeing-up" of urban space. The congestion of the old walking city was reduced, and the streetcar provided, overall, a less densely populated metropolis at the same time that it enabled cities to experience dramatic population growth. The space included in the metropolitan area increased at a much faster rate than did the population.

In the process of expansion, the streetcar city sorted itself out into different zones. A distinct central business district emerged. In Chicago, after the great fire of 1871, houses, churches, and other features of residential neighborhoods disappeared from downtown. Other areas of the city specialized in facilities for work, housing, recreation, transportation, and commercial use. The residential neighborhoods also sorted themselves out by social or economic class and, to a large extent, along ethnic and racial lines.

The resident of the new city of specialized zones connected to each other by streetcar tracks needed a map of the metropolis to provide an image of the city as a whole. In the walking city, residents usually did not need maps because they were familiar with all parts of town. In the streetcar city, however, one knew, on the basis of personal contact, only a few of the residential areas, the downtown area, and the strips along the streetcar routes, which one used. To visit another area of the city, to ride another streetcar line, or to locate places off one's usual beat called for a map of the city. It is of interest that the earliest street maps of Chicago, prepared especially for residents, appeared just after the introduction of streetcars. These maps clearly marked the routes of the horse-car lines.

The transformation of the walking city into the streetcar city was a gradual development that took several generations to complete. The process had not fully run its course when the automobile appeared as an alternative means of intraurban transportation. Like the streetcar, two of its early functions were to take residents on holiday drives to the greenbelts surrounding the metropolitan area and to ferry visitors back and forth between railroad stations and hotels. As in the first transformation of the city, the automobile led to a greatly expanded urban area; it changed the character of the urban landscape; and it reduced still further the density of urban settlement.

Chapter 4 noted how the advent of cars turned the streets into traffic arteries and parking lots. It also noted how garages steadily marched from alley quarters at the rear of lots to places of honor at the front of the houses. If sidewalks and alleys on occasion disappeared, the common space at the front of residential lots spread in extent, surrounding the house on all sides. The expanding landscape of one lot merged into that of the neighbors and produced an impression of individual homes lined up like flowers in a garden of common space.

Observers of the new automobile suburbs were struck by the extent to which the new communities had sorted out the various land uses. Zoning codes specified the size, shape, nature, and value of the residential units and absolutely prohibited the intrusion into these neighborhoods of commercial, institutional, or industrial structures. The zones for work also had their buildings planted on lawns and set back from the street in industrial areas, office parks, and shopping malls. The latter phenomenon in many ways re-created the life of the street in an enclosed or in an indoor setting. Some malls went so far as to reintroduce street musicians, vending carts, and neighborhood fairs within their confines.

The automobile marched into the old streetcar city as well as into the surrounding suburbs. Just as the Chicago Fire largely wiped out the old walking city and hastened the triumph of an urban plan based on streetcar tracks, so the urban renewal (or urban removal) program sponsored by the federal government in the post-World War II era hastened the triumph of the internal combustion engine in the heart of the city. In the 1940s and 1950s, buses replaced streetcars, at first using overhead trolley wires and electric motors, but soon also turning to the internal combustion engines. By 1960, wide paths were being cut through the streetcar neighborhoods to make way for urban expressways. The old car tracks were removed as shopping and entertainment centers migrated from downtown to suburban malls, thereby reducing the central business district to a large office park ringed by a variety of parking facilities.

The expressway system on the map recalls the ornamental garage doors in the suburbs. Both signify the triumph of the automobile city. New maps and a new approach to urban cartography were demanded by residents of the new automobile metropolis. The expressway system became the basic frame of reference for people using maps. The territory of the metropolis extended over vastly enlarged areas, tied together by highways and superhighways that led across town and around the town as well as downtown. The city, as a political unity, became locked in a Sargasso Sea of suburbs stretching to the borders of the new metropolitan map. The center of the new urban plan could usually be found at the interchange between the expressways at the gateway to the central business district.

The ramifications of the changes wrought by the transportation revolution can be located on the maps of nearly every American community. In some ways, they are magnified by the experience of large metropolitan areas. But few towns fail to exhibit traces of the changes whereby walking communities became streetcar towns, and then were transformed, within memory, by the automobile. The "three cities" mode of analysis may inform a discussion of the changing nature of villages and rural areas as well. It has explanatory power whether one is focusing on the history of a house or a school, a church or a factory, a fire station or a zoo.

As one walks through the cityscape, or examines the maps with care, one realizes that the triumph of the new is never complete. Relic features of the former eras dot the landscape, and some features of the earlier town plans resist change like monadnocks. These are the features that grab us as we take our walks. They remind us of the continuities that exist in a community in the midst of constant change.

The cityscape, Martin Meyerson and Barbara Terrett observed in 1957, was like a crazy quilt. Both were haphazard yet planned.

Every metropolis is characteristically a practical patchwork of income, race, and age; of private and public ownership; of a new and the old; of identical and of mixed land uses; of households, firms, and institutions whose interests converge, diverge, conflict with, and complement each other. . . All of these competitions draw together, just as the patches do in the quilt, and provide a perceptible fabric. Compromises, conflicts, congruities, incongruities, agreements, and disagreements in behavior and interest come together in that colorful made-do, the metropolis." (From *Metropolis in Ferment, The Annals of the American Academy of Political and Social Science*, volume 314, 1957, p. 1)

Types of Public Places

Leaving the maps at the table, it is time to push our chairs aside and journey through the community to look for public places. When we return, we might note how the town plan ties all of these special areas together into a functioning community. We might even use felt-tipped pens of different colors to highlight on the maps the different types of public places found as we survey the community.

The federal presence. The mailbox on the porch, in the lobby, or down the road reminds us that the federal government claims a space for every house and building in a community. Federal laws and regulations specify that mailboxes must be present and limit their use to "official business." The post office in most communities is a hub of activities sponsored by the national government. The main post office is usually worth visiting as a representative type of public building. Its location, its architecture, its inscriptions, its art, its posters, and even its landscaping often register the nature and purpose of the federal government.

In many cities, the post office building is also used for other governmental activities, and the story of the post office in a local community is often an important window to its history. The relationship between post offices and national defense was especially apparent during the World Wars, but the presence of facilities for national defense in local communities also extends to highways, schools (National Defense Education Act), airports, and military installations themselves. Many communities were forts in their early days or received batteries, magazines, or radar sites at later dates in their histories.

The earliest public works built by the national government were lighthouses. These are still landmarks for many communities, but the federal activities to improve navigation, provide land grants for railroads, and build highways, bridges, flood control devices, and airports should not be overlooked as one makes an inventory of the federal presence. If one includes grants, charters, regulations, subsidies, and tax write-offs, the input of the national government might be discerned on almost every building in a community. And, as chapter 3 pointed out, the system of Congressional land division still affects almost all of the land once owned by the national government.

City halls, courthouses, and capitols. The focal point for civic life in most communities revolves around the city hall, the county courthouse, or, in fifty cases, a state capitol. Although these ornamental buildings are sometimes located at the edge of a town, their normal situation is near the heart of the city, in the historical core, or on a geographically favored site at the top of a hill. As centers of government and civic life, they are important places in the dynamics of a community, but their importance usually goes beyond their functional aspects. They are symbolic statements of the power and aspirations of the polis. Especially in the nineteenth century, it was fashionable to make these buildings look like palaces, to adorn them with ornaments, statues, inscriptions, and, in some cases, stained glass celebrating the history of the community.

In towns where there has been a succession of municipal buildings or courthouses, it is possible to use the changing size and style of the structures to say something about the development of the place and the changing roles that government was expected to play. It is also possible to relate these governmental buildings to the "three cities" concept. In the walking city, they were often indistinguishable from neighboring structures, or they might be housed in buildings with several uses. Chicago's first city hall, for example, was located above a marketplace and shared quarters with several other local institutions.

The streetcar city saw the elaboration and specialization of the city hall as a structure. Since all the streetcar lines led downtown, the public buildings at the urban core were seen and visited by almost every citizen. Architects and governmental officials saw the buildings as conveying a message to citizens and visitors alike. As the discussion in chapter 4 indicated, the buildings in streetcar cities carried a variety of forms and decorations to engage the pedestrians. With the coming of the automobile, the buildings became more functional. The center of the city also lost much of its purpose as a central meeting place when the streetcar tracks were removed. Many citizens of the automobile metropolis avoided going downtown where it was difficult to park and traffic was very congested. The newer governmental buildings looked more like office buildings as they lost the old pedestrian audience. In some cases, they were even relocated to park-like settings at the edge of the community where cars could be accommodated more easily. In any case, elaborate decorations, inscriptions, and memorials became a thing of the past.

The new governmental buildings were designed more for the comfort of those who worked in them than for any type of symbolic statement about the aspirations of the community. Nevertheless, many of the older buildings have been maintained and restored as civic ornaments and reminders of a past era. As such they often provide a unique opportunity for students of public places to make connections between the past and the present, between individual lives and public places, and between the local experience and national ideals.

Public service structures. The symbolic qualities of the dignified old court-houses and city halls were often echoed in a variety of supplementary public structures. This was especially true for police stations, firehouses, and waterworks. As these municipal services were added in the nineteenth century, the specialized buildings served as extensions of the governmental presence from the center of the community to outlying neighborhoods. They not only provided essential services, they also announced the presence of the local government. Thus they were decked out in formal architectural dress, labeled with inscriptions and insignia, and located in places of prominence.

In many ways, the development of these satellite structures paralleled the transformation of the walking city into the streetcar city. As the original settlement extended its territory and divided up the metropolis into a series of specialized areas and neighborhoods, the functions of government were often compartmentalized as well. Each district needed its own police precinct, firehouse, market hall, and pumping station, indicating that people no longer thought of the community as a homogeneous entity but as an aggregate of parts pulled together by a central core.

The public structures in a neighborhood usually emphasized their direct connection to the historical core. Perhaps this explains the importance of inscriptions, symbols, flags, uniforms, standardized equipment, official colors, and other devices that forcefully reminded local residents of their ties to the civic polity as a whole.

The development of the automobile city and the functionalism of its architecture reduced, to some extent, the symbolic function of these structures. Modern technology has made it possible to remove public buildings almost entirely from the residential neighborhoods. In the automobile suburb, they are often located in out-of-the-way places, the availability of the urban services being simply taken for granted. The only such structure that seemed particularly adapted to the automobile way of life was the water tank. It was large enough to be clearly visible from the road, and it became the practice to paint the community's name on the tank in large letters so motorists would know which town they were passing by.

To the student of local history, the various public structures for promoting public safety and for distributing public services record the impact of technology on the nature and functions of government. They also document the web of connections that tie the locality into a larger community.

Cultural institutions. Public places for the transmission of culture, for education and edification, are essential parts of a community structure. Churches
and schools, libraries and museums, not only foster the development of an
individual but also stress participation in a larger community as well. Cultural institutions are encouraged by the government, usually exempted from
taxes, and are supported by individuals in a community as a public duty.
To the student of community history, they make two fundamental points
about the nature of the American experience.

The first point is the multicultural nature of American society. Not everyone
in the community is expected to belong to the same church, attend the
same school, or patronize the same museum or library. Although there are
governmental systems of schools and libraries supported by general taxation,
there are places for parallel institutions of a more parochial nature as well.
There is a feeling that communities will be richer if they include a variety
of traditions, and the typical American town includes people from several
different religious groups. Although some pressures have encouraged a common educational system for children, the argument for a unitary educational
establishment has seldom been pushed to include higher education. The
cultural and educational institutions of a variety of traditions have, by and
large, flourished in American communities, and the trend over time has
been to increase this diversity. Cities often take pride in the number of different religious buildings, schools, and ethnic restaurants they can list in the
guidebooks for visitors.

A second way in which a consideration of cultural institutions in a community serves the interest of nearby history is to point to roots and origins
beyond the community itself, back in time and across the seas. To understand the architecture of a church, the curriculum of a school, the holdings
of a local library, or exhibits in a particular museum, one usually needs some
knowledge of Western civilization and of world history. The design of a college campus, the plan of a religious institution, the way things are arranged
in libraries and museums, all forcefully remind us that local history is only
a particular manifestation of much broader forces and much older traditions.

Thus cultural institutions as public places serve as important reminders
of the diversity that exists in a community and its place in a broader context. These are important elements in a civic education and explain why
critics of the automobile city lament the trend toward the homogenization
of these institutions and the uniform look of their buildings.

Market places, commercial structures, and accommodations. Some students of the origins of modern communities have emphasized the key role of outsiders in bringing new goods, new ideas, and new ways of doing things. Cities and towns at the dawn of the modern age considered the accommodation of visitors and the encouragement of commerce as two of the principal reasons for their existence. Special laws and regulations, as well as special public places, were developed to fulfill these functions. A map of the downtown area of any city will document how these areas are still largely devoted to the accommodation of visitors and the exchange of goods and ideas.

At the most basic level, places for visitors to eat, drink, and sleep have been enduring features of downtown life. These places have usually served important functions for the residents of the community as well as for visitors. The early inns were centers of community life, and the modern motel has its special rooms for community groups to meet and for families to celebrate weddings and anniversaries. A history of laws dealing with public accommodations in any state or community will illustrate how restaurants, hotels, and even places of amusement or entertainment have been defined as semipublic places and accorded special legal treatment.

Although places of accommodation in America were almost always owned by private individuals or groups, places for the exchange of goods were often established as governmental facilities. Frequently, market squares and market halls were owned by the municipalities and were given special legal status. Banks, shops, stores, and warehouses were also, by extension, given the privileges and responsibilities of public places. The role of modern cities in erecting stadiums, convention halls, trade centers, and airports continues a function expressed at an earlier period in public wharves, docks, market halls, bridges, and even pastures. Thus the student of public places must not overlook the ways in which communities have encouraged the accommodation of visitors and the transporting, storage, and exchange of goods.

The automobile city has transformed the nature of public accommodations and commercial exchange in American communities. As travel between communities shifted from rails to the highways, hotels and restaurants found that travelers often preferred to stop for eating and sleeping out of town along the road. Soon an entire landscape was developed to serve the needs of the motorists: fast-food restaurants, motels, and automobile service stations. Shopping malls and stores set back off the street with large parking lots in front were parallel developments in districts for retail trade. Wholesaling and warehousing also relocated, in large measure to specialized "industrial districts" conveniently located near places where interstate highways came together.

Parks. The public park, as we know it, developed as a response to the streetcar city of the mid-nineteenth century. Antecedents can be found in the open spaces such as squares, commons, marketplaces, and landings provided in the early town plans of the walking city, but the development of special landscaped areas for the enjoyment of all citizens was not common until after 1853, the year Central Park was established in New York City. Boston Common, dating from 1634, had from its inception some functions of outdoor recreation, but these shared the space in walking-city style with other land uses: pasture, parade grounds, and field of assembly.

Parks were first advocated as ways to address some urban problems resulting from the physical congestion of the walking city: crowded housing, poor lighting, foul air, and the absence of a natural environment. With the introduction of streetcars, citizens could reach the edge of the city where enough land was available for houses with gardens ("streetcar suburbs"), for cemeteries (landscaped "rural" burial grounds), and for public parks.

It was soon discovered that one large park was not adequate to meet the varying needs of the whole urban population. First parkways and boulevards were advocated as extensions, links, and entryways for the large parks. By the 1890s, park advocates suggested smaller parks, one for each of the new neighborhoods into which the city was divided. In 1892, an influential study of park needs in Boston suggested that all the individual parklands in that city be combined into one administrative system. Most American cities soon followed this example, sometimes making the park district into a separate metropolitan agency, at other times placing the parks under a department of the city government.

At the same time, patterns of public use changed the whole concept of parks. Settlement houses in the 1890s created special playgrounds for children and then urged cities to provide these areas as a municipal responsibility. It was natural to build playgrounds in parks, and soon many older parks were re-designed to provide athletic fields, gymnasiums, swimming pools, meeting rooms, and educational facilities. The neighborhood park became a community center. The regional and central parks, meanwhile, expanded their functions as places for zoos, art galleries, museums, conservatories, and formal gardens to serve the entire metropolitan area.

County governments took over the park idea and placed it in a more rural setting. County parks were largely a response to the widespread ownership of automobiles in the 1920s. In 1895, there apparently was only one county park, in Essex, New Jersey, but by the 1930s they numbered in the hundreds. State and national parks had their origins in preserving exceptional natural features for public access, such as the hot springs in Arkansas (1832) or the geysers in Yellowstone (1872), but again the automobile encouraged their expansion and adaptation to a variety of recreational uses.

Thus one could divide the history of the public park movement in the United States into four periods: the early era of the walking city, a period of squares, commons, parade grounds, and landings; the building of large central parks and parkway networks in the streetcar cities from the 1850s to the 1890s; the emergence of the neighborhood park and city-wide park systems between 1890 and 1930 at the height of the streetcar cities; and the impact of the automobile on parks beginning in the 1920s and continuing up to the present.

Common space. There is one more type of public place, one that does not show up on maps but is largely a product of the streetcar and the automobile cities. It is really not public space since it is private property. The person who has best caught the significance of this space is Gregory Conniff, an artist and photographer. Coining the term, "common ground," he notes that it "is the space around American homes." It is the land between a building and the lot line, especially that part of a lot that is in public view. These were the spaces made possible as the city spread over a larger and larger territory. And the expanding metropolis, was, as we have seen, a direct result of streetcars and automobiles.

The common spaces are really transition zones between public and private spaces. Conniff's reflections on the civic meaning of this space are a good place to conclude our survey to public places and evaluate our efforts. Guidebooks, he notes, usually avoid most of the real world, the world of nearby history.

They set themselves to the easy task of drawing attention to distinguishable phenomena and ignore the connective tissue that holds the world together. They reinforce the notion that what is worth pursuing is somehow never where we live. . . .

What I have called *Common Ground*. . . is a primary place, a personal landscape. It is home ground. At the same time it is open to the view of others . . . a point of departure and a place of return. (From *Common Ground*, 1985, p. xii).

Suggested Readings

Gregory Conniff's *Common Ground* is the first of a three-volume field guide, via striking photographs, "to the community of being that comes from sharing a particular place" (New Haven, Conn.: Yale University Press, 1985). The same press has issued *Common Landscape of America, 1580 to 1845* by John R. Stilgoe (1982), a book of a much different character and one which offers a much different interpretive framework for looking at the structure of early American communities. It is especially good for anyone with a project centered on an American community in the Colonial or early national period. It emphasizes the Old World background and sees the early American landscape as a reflection of late medieval or early modern ways of life. With more than 400 pages of text, it covers a myriad of subjects from lighthouses to fences. Unfortunately there is, as yet, no subsequent volume to carry the story beyond the 1840s.

Most beginning students of nearby history are more comfortable starting with the present and working back from there. Here, a helpful little book comes to mind in the "Building Watchers" series sponsored by the National Trust for Historic Preservation. *Built in the U.S.A: American Buildings from Airports to Zoos,* edited by Diane Maddex (Washington, D.C.: The Preservation Press, 1985) includes more than forty types of buildings, each discussed by a different authority. Somewhere between two and eight bibliographical suggestions are given for each building type.

The outstanding volume on *The Federal Presence,* by Lois A. Craig and the staff of the Federal Architecture Project, deals with "Architecture, Politics, and National Design" (Cambridge, Mass.: MIT Press, 1984). *America's City Halls* by William L. Lebovich (Washington, D.C.: The Preservation Press, 1984) is a wonderful survey of about a hundred outstanding examples in photographs and text. Charles King Hoyt's *Public, Municipal, and Community Buildings* (New York: McGraw-Hill, 1980) surveys the field for architects but can be profitably used by anyone.

There are a number of studies of courthouses in various states. One of the best of these volumes extends its coverage to jails and other municipal buildings as well: Willard B. Robinson, *The People's Architecture* (Austin: Texas State Historical Association, 1983). Rebecca Zurier's *The American Firehouse: An Architectural and Social History* (New York: Abbeville Press, 1982) documents, often without conscious explanation, the power of the "three cities" concept. It is burdended, however, by a polemical tone.

Perry R. Duis, *The Saloon; Public Drinking in Chicago and Boston, 1880-1920* (Urbana: University of Illinois Press, 1983) is, in contrast, a splendid scholarly study of a semipublic place in the streetcar city. Chapter 3 on "The Saloon and the Public Neighborhood," especially the comments on the institution as an extension of the home, is germane to the focus of this chapter. The opening pages of the book discuss different types of urban spaces: private, public, and semipublic.

As the reader will have gathered, there is much to be gained by looking at public places from the perspective of the arts. The most helpful volume for beginning students is *Place Makers: Public Art that Tells You Where You Are* by Ronald Lee Fleming and Renata van Tscharner (New York: Hastings House, 1981).

The concept of "three cities" presented here is a distillation of two decades of reading and looking. If one wishes to try to trace some these ideas to their source, and to note where the ideas have been twisted in one way or another, two profitable guides would be Sam Bass Warner, *Streetcar Suburbs: The Process of Growth in Boston* (second edition, Cambridge, Mass.: Harvard University Press, 1978) and *A History of Urban America* by Charles N. Glaab and A. Theodore Brown (third edition, New York: Macmillan, 1983).

·Appendix A·

Working With Time

IN RECONSTRUCTING THE HISTORY OF MONUMENTS, buildings, or other public places, researchers will want to develop a list of important events connected with the subject at hand. As they read the primary and secondary sources in the research stage of the project, they can record these "notable events" on 3-by-5 inch note cards, leaving the top line blank except for the date. When the first round of research has been completed, placing the note cards in chronological order will create a chronology or basic structure for the project. But researchers should not stop here, for this is only the first step in working with time.

The next stage in the research is to look for gaps in one's knowledge, and this can often be done by transferring the dates from the chronology onto a time line such as that suggested on page 67. Long periods of inactivity or gaps in the story will show up vividly on a time line where the years are measured off on a consistent scale. Further research can fill in these gaps or explain why there was such a long stretch of uneventful years.

A time line is also helpful in the next stage of a research project, organizing the material. Note that the sample on page 117 has the scale of years down the center of the sheet. The list of significant events can be recorded on the left side of the page, leaving the other side free for trying out several periodization schemes. This process is pure interpretation, for by dividing the time line into periods, one is making judgments about the meaning and purpose of the development. It is true that a subjective element was also present in finding the sources to use and in selecting those events that appeared to be significant. But dividing the chronology into periods brings one face to face with interpretive issues. What events serve as turning points in the story? What labels shall be given to various periods? Do some events not fit well into the account? What shall we do with these "outsiders"? Suppress them or reduce them to "insignificant events"?

The process of periodization usually brings to light the interpretive frame the researcher has been using. Thus it also provides an opportunity to consider alternative modes of analysis. One can cover the right-hand side of the time line with blank sheets of paper and "try out" a variety of periodization schemes. Beginning students are sometimes surprised to learn that the periods into which a historical account is divided do not appear as "givens" but are created by the historian.

The right-hand side of the time line is also useful as the researcher tries to relate what is happening in the particular story to the larger context of urban, state, national, or international affairs. Key events from these realms can be recorded side-by-side with those developed out of the nearby history. It is a good idea to use several different sets of comparative data as one explores the various contexts into which the history of a public place may be set.

A TIMELINE OF CHICAGO

DATE	EVENT		PERIODIZATION BY URBAN TRANSPORTATION
		1750	
1763	Treaty of Paris		
		1775	
1779	DuSable settlement		
1783	Treaty of Paris		
			Frontier Paths and Trails: to 1830
1803	Fort Dearborn	1800	
		1825	
1830	First streets and lots		
			Walking City 1830-1860
1848	Canal and railroad	1850	
1859	First streetcar		
1871	Chicago Fire		
		1875	
1885	First skyscraper		
1893	Columbian Exposition		
		1900	Streetcar City 1860-1949
1909	Burnham Plan		
1919	Race Riot		
		1925	
1933	Century of Progress Fair		
1949	Congress Expressway begun	1950	
1968	Year of Protest		Automobile City 1949-present
1976	Mayor Daley's death	1975	
1978	Byrne elected mayor		
		2000	

·Appendix B·

Working With Space

ALMOST EVERY PROJECT ON THE HISTORY OF PUBLIC places will benefit from the use of maps. Cartographic materials have often been used to illustrate historical accounts, to provide a general understanding of the nature of a region, to note the location of key places, or, in the case of old maps, to serve as markers for the passage of years. The historian of public places, however, will want to use maps as primary sources in a much more active way. One works with space by asking questions of the maps, searching for significant details, systematically analyzing them from a variety of perspectives, and comparing one map with another.

The following checklist is designed to assist this type of research. Not every point will be of interest in every project, nor will it apply to every map. Each category, however, should be considered when analyzing a particular map. It can be quickly passed over if it proves not to be of use. Maps have a way of raising questions that have not been asked. They also often alert us to data we might have overlooked or point to relationships that we had not thought of before.

Using Maps as Primary Sources: A Checklist

I. The Cartographic Context
  A. Bibliographical Data
    1. The title or titles of the map
    2. The publisher or cartographer
    3. The date of the map
      a. The date of the data and/or the base map
      b. The date of drawing
      c. The date of publication
    4. The place of publication (or deposit, if a manuscript map)
  B. The Map in its Setting
    1. Who made it?
    2. For what purpose?

       3. For what audience?

       4. When was it made?

       5. Where was it drawn?

   C. The Rhetorical Elements

       1. The type of publication

       2. Technical quality

       3. Accuracy

       4. Design characteristics

       5. Cultural values on the map

          a. Explicit

          b. Implicit

   D. The Map in its Families or Categories (the importance of seeing a map as one of a group)

       1. Of place

       2. Of date

       3. Of function

       4. Of maker and/or publisher

   E. The Map in its Individuality

       1. Historical associations

       2. Changes on the map

       3. Provenance

II. Reading the Map

   A. The Standard Cartographic Elements

       1. Direction

       2. Scale

       3. Grid system (coordinates)

       4. Symbols

          a. Key

          b. Color

          c. Boundaries

   B. The Map as a Whole: Principals of Orientation

       1. Land and water

       2. Grid system

       3. Boundaries and districts

       4. Landforms

       5. Routes and transportation facilities

       6. Land use data

       7. Landmarks

III. Reading the Map: Physical Features

   A. Hydrography

       1. Bodies of water

       2. River and streams

3. Drainage patterns
4. Drainage divides and basins
5. Seasonal variation
6. Engineering (see "Cultural Features," IV., part B)
B. Topography
1. The portrayal of relief
2. Landforms
3. Relationship to sea level: elevation
4. Physiographic regions
C. Soils and Geology
1. Soil types
2. Surface geology
3. Outcropping
4. Economic geology
5. Ground water supplies
D. Vegetation
1. Natural vegetation
2. Current vegetation
3. Tree cover
4. Land use categories based on vegetation: urban, suburban, agricultural, open space, natural preserves
5. Ecosystems

IV. Reading the Map: Cultural Features
A. Land Division
1. Surveyors' lines and points
2. Systems of land division
3. Basic units: townships and sections
4. Subdivisions and lots
5. Field patterns
6. Reserves
7. Special use areas
8. Corrections
B. Civil Engineering
1. Dams and flood control systems
2. Canals and locks
3. Harbor improvements and breakwaters
4. Bridges
5. Drainage systems
6. Landfill areas
7. Topographic changes
C. Transportation
1. Water routes
2. Land corridors

3. Arterial streets or intercity roads
4. Railroads
   a. Mainlines
   b. Short lines and belt systems
   c. Switching yards
   d. Terminals
   e. Junctions and crossings
   f. Interchange with other transportation facilities
6. Roads and highways
   a. Type: local, state, U.S., interstate systems
   b. Patterns: nodes, hubs, radials, grids
   c. Pavement type
   d. Facilities to aid movement of goods and people
7. Streets in cities and towns
   a. Urban planning: formal, grid, irregular
   b. Orientation of local streets
   c. Subdivision units
   d. Gaps, irregularities, and breaks in the pattern
   e. Plazas
   f. Alleys
8. Airports
   a. Type: local, regional, international
   b. Location - physical site
   c. Location - relationship to population distribution
   d. Connection to other types of transportation facilities
D. Land Use and Economic Features
   1. Agricultural land use
      a. Fields and field patterns
      b. Range and grazing lands
      c. Orchards and timber lands
      d. Storage and transportation facilities
      e. Processing plants
   2. Extractive industries
      a. Mines
      b. Quarries
      c. Sand and gravel pits
      d. Spoil dumps
      e. Forestry
      f. Fishing
      g. Support facilities
   3. Industrial and manufacturing facilities
      a. Individual sites and complexes
      b. Zones and districts
      c. Transportation facilities

       d. Sources of energy and raw materials: stockpiles
       e. Housing the workers
   4. Commercial facilities
       a. Local shopping and service areas
       b. Regional shopping and service areas
       c. Central business districts
       d. Warehouse and distribution facilities
       e. Offices
   5. Public administrative and service areas
       a. Governmental buildings, courthouses
       b. Public safety facilities: police, fire protection, jails
       c. Schools, libraries, and education institutions
       d. Post offices
       e. Hospitals and social service facilities
       f. Cemeteries and burial grounds
   6. Recreational facilities
       a. Parks and playgrounds
       b. Nature preserves
       c. Golf courses and country clubs
       d. Racetracks, yacht clubs, etc.
       e. Stadiums
   7. Religious and cultural institutions
       a. Churches, synagogues, mosques, and shrines
       b. Museums and galleries
       c. Theaters
       d. Historic sites and landmarks
   8. Utilities
       a. Power generation and distribution
       b. Water storage, purification, and distribution
       c. Sewers and water treatment
       d. Communication facilities

V. Map Interpretation
  A. Patterns of Distribution
    1. Population and settlement patterns
    2. Economic activities
    3. Open spaces and vegetation types
    4. Land use and zoning
    5. Land division and ownership
  B. Interactions
    1. Land and water
    2. Physical features and cultural features
    3. Between physiographic regions or ecological areas
    4. Urban-suburban-rural interrelationships

    5. Transportation facilities and settlement patterns
    6. Plans and circumstances
C. Clues to Larger Meanings
    1. Place names (ethnic, historical, cultural, and geographical references)
    2. The life cycle on the map
    3. Economic cycle: raw materials, production, distribution, consumption, disposal
    4. Identified features as parts of larger complexes
    5. Beats and personal associations
    6. Groups of people: social, economic, racial, ethnic, and religious characteristics
D. The Time Factor
    1. Breaks: development over time
    2. Relic features
    3. Vacant lands
    4. Recycled features
    5. Present trends
    6. Future plans and directions
E. Geographic Concepts
    1. Site
    2. Situation
    3. Nodality: central places
    4. Hinterland
    5. Complementary trade relationships
    6. Break-in-bulk points
    7. Districts and regions

·Appendix C·
Working With People

BY DEFINITION, BOTH PUBLIC PLACES AND HISTORY
itself center on people. Along with time and space, people form an essential ingredient in any study of nearby history. Spaces become places because
human beings use them and shape them according to their cultural needs.
Time, as it exists in its natural state, as the rhythm of the seasons or as
an astronomical event, is of little interest to historians. But when it relates
to individuals as personal time in a life cycle, or to groups as civic time
or as cultural expression, it becomes the very stuff of history. By comparing
the lives and works of people over time, it is possible to discern the elements of change and continuity between one point in the past and another.

In planning a historical investigation, it is usually a good idea to start
with people and then to qualify the topic by limiting its scope in time and
space. One can think of people as individuals or as members of a group.
The first illustration notes how the groups to which an individual belongs
may be conceived in progressively larger spheres. Each circle could also be
divided into various subgroups by gender, age, economic class, social status,
occupation, religious persuasion, membership in various clubs or organiza-
tions, and so on. Of course, these overlap and are often themselves subject
to change over time. Historians need to consider at the very outset of a
project which ways of thinking about people will best serve their research
needs.

The next illustration provides an example of how researchers might han-
dle the people dimension in a nearby history project. The time line supplies a framework for relating the life of a person in one generation to the
life of a person in the next. The public place that connects these individuals
is Hull-House, the celebrated social settlement on the Near West Side of
Chicago. The "people cards," noting how the individuals moved from place
to place in their careers, summarize each person's life. After such a structure
is firmly in mind, one can use the various ways in which we divide people

into groups to see which of these approaches will be most useful. Will the various approaches help develop some themes or answer questions raised by the topic at hand?

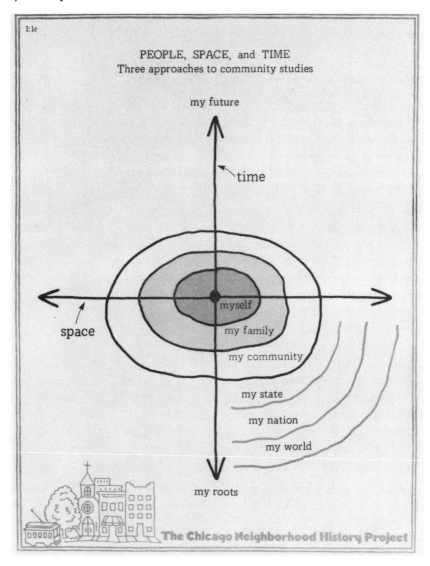

PEORLE, SPACE, and TIME
Three approaches to community studies

my future

time

myself
my family
my community

my state

my nation

my world

space

my roots

The Chicago Neighborhood History Project

A PEOPLE FILE

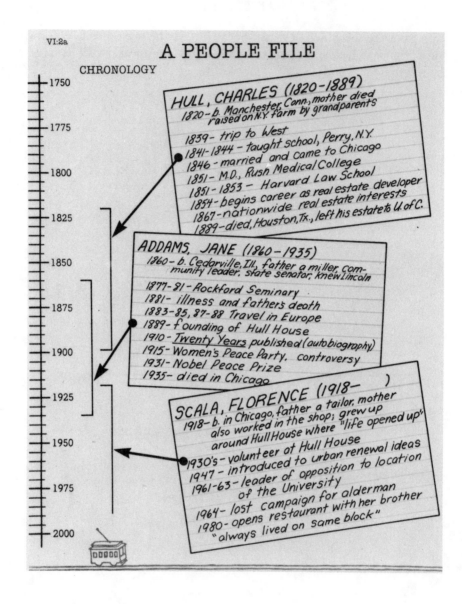

1750

1775

1800

1825

1850

1875

1900

1925

1950

1975

2000

HULL, CHARLES (1820-1889)
1820- b. Manchester, Conn., mother died
raised on N.Y. farm by grandparents

1839- trip to West
1841-1844 - taught school, Perry, N.Y.
1846- married and came to Chicago
1851- M.D., Rush Medical College
1851-1853 - Harvard Law School
1854- begins career as real estate developer
1867- nationwide real estate interests
1889- died, Houston, Tx., left his estate to U. of C.

ADDAMS, JANE (1860-1935)
1860- b. Cedarville, Ill., father a miller, community leader; state senator; knew Lincoln

1877-81- Rockford Seminary
1881- illness and father's death
1883-85, 87-88 Travel in Europe
1889- founding of Hull House
1910- _Twenty Years_ published (autobiography)
1915- Women's Peace Party, controversy
1931- Nobel Peace Prize
1935- died in Chicago

SCALA, FLORENCE (1918-   )
1918- b. in Chicago, father a tailor, mother
also worked in the shop; grew up
around Hull House where "life opened up"

1930's- volunteer at Hull House
1947- introduced to urban renewal ideas
1961-63- leader of opposition to location
of the University
1964- lost campaign for alderman
1980- opens restaurant with her brother
"always lived on same block"

·Appendix D·

Formats for Nearby History

AT SOME POINT WHILE THE RESEARCH IS UNDER WAY, IF not at the very inception of a project in nearby history, one must decide on a format for presenting the fruits of one's labors. Without a means of recording or sharing your findings, the effort will soon be lost. Again, by definition, historians are those who study the past and give their findings to an audience. Without the audience, there is no history.

There are at least five major ways in which the history of public places may be presented to the general public: the formal paper, an exhibit, an oral report, a slide presentation, and a walking tour. There are many good manuals on writing a formal paper, but it is often difficult to locate some guide for the more informal types of presentations.

The following charts might be helpful as one "blocks out" a schedule for a project. Note that in every case there are many more steps to go through after the research phase of the project has been completed. Should further suggestions be needed, one could consult the large manual from which the charts were taken: *People, Space, and Time: An Introduction to Community History for Schools* by Gerald A. Danzer and Lawrence W. McBride (Washington, D.C.: University Press of America for the Chicago Metro History Fair, 1985). These materials were developed as part of the Chicago Neighborhood History Project with the support of the National Endowment for the Humanities.

127

HOW TO DO AN EXHIBIT

I. Getting an Idea
  A. Think about a topic
  B. Think about items to display
  C. Think about a layout

II. Research
  A. Background reading
  B. Identify major themes
  C. Collect items to display

III. Synthesis
  A. Choose a title
  B. Select items to display
  C. Develop a layout

IV. Blueprint Stage
  A. Layout sketch
  B. Check dimensions
  C. Criticism
  D. Revise as necessary

V. Writing
  A. Theme cards
  B. Identification labels
  C. Acknowledgement card

VI. Construction
  A. Gather materials
  B. Mount display items
  C. Add theme cards, labels, title

VII. Grand Opening
  A. Receive visitors
  B. Use speaking skills when explaining exhibit
  C. Be prepared to answer questions

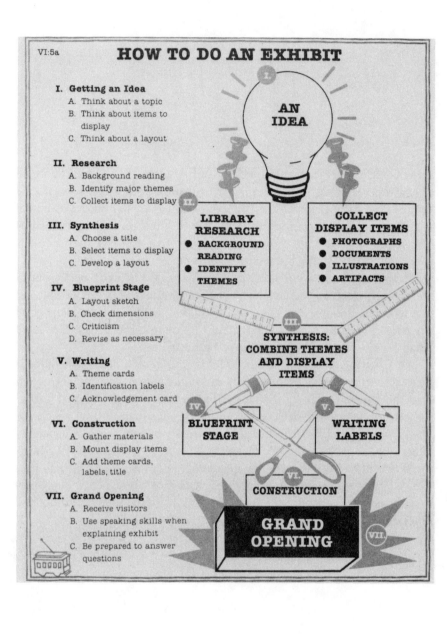

HOW TO DO AN ORAL REPORT

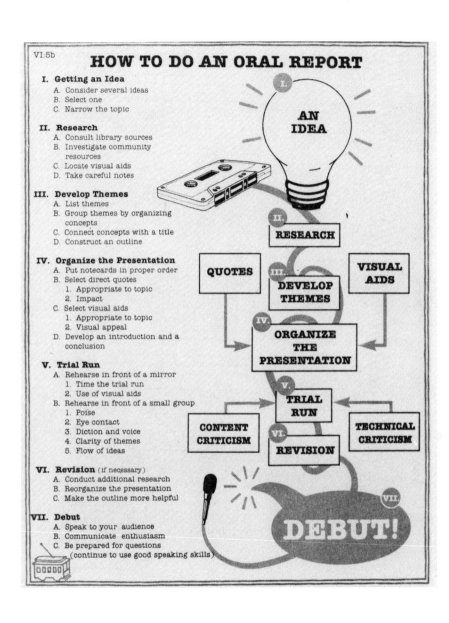

I. Getting an Idea
  A. Consider several ideas
  B. Select one
  C. Narrow the topic

II. Research
  A. Consult library sources
  B. Investigate community resources
  C. Locate visual aids
  D. Take careful notes

III. Develop Themes
  A. List themes
  B. Group themes by organizing concepts
  C. Connect concepts with a title
  D. Construct an outline

IV. Organize the Presentation
  A. Put notecards in proper order
  B. Select direct quotes
    1. Appropriate to topic
    2. Impact
  C. Select visual aids
    1. Appropriate to topic
    2. Visual appeal
  D. Develop an introduction and a conclusion

V. Trial Run
  A. Rehearse in front of a mirror
    1. Time the trial run
    2. Use of visual aids
  B. Rehearse in front of a small group
    1. Poise
    2. Eye contact
    3. Diction and voice
    4. Clarity of themes
    5. Flow of ideas

VI. Revision (if necessary)
  A. Conduct additional research
  B. Reorganize the presentation
  C. Make the outline more helpful

VII. Debut
  A. Speak to your audience
  B. Communicate enthusiasm
  C. Be prepared for questions
    (continue to use good speaking skills)

I. AN IDEA

II. RESEARCH

QUOTES

III. DEVELOP THEMES

VISUAL AIDS

IV. ORGANIZE THE PRESENTATION

V. TRIAL RUN

CONTENT CRITICISM

VI. REVISION

TECHNICAL CRITICISM

VII. DEBUT!

HOW TO DO A SLIDE PRESENTATION

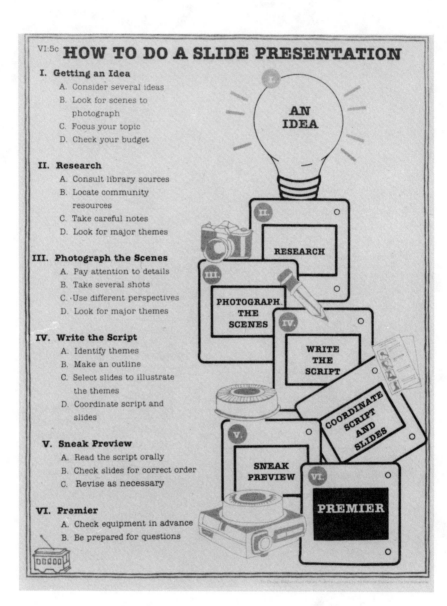

I. Getting an Idea
- A. Consider several ideas
- B. Look for scenes to photograph
- C. Focus your topic
- D. Check your budget

II. Research
- A. Consult library sources
- B. Locate community resources
- C. Take careful notes
- D. Look for major themes

III. Photograph the Scenes
- A. Pay attention to details
- B. Take several shots
- C. Use different perspectives
- D. Look for major themes

IV. Write the Script
- A. Identify themes
- B. Make an outline
- C. Select slides to illustrate the themes
- D. Coordinate script and slides

V. Sneak Preview
- A. Read the script orally
- B. Check slides for correct order
- C. Revise as necessary

VI. Premier
- A. Check equipment in advance
- B. Be prepared for questions

AN
IDEA

RESEARCH

PHOTOGRAPH
THE
SCENES

WRITE
THE
SCRIPT

COORDINATE
SCRIPT
AND
SLIDES

SNEAK
PREVIEW

PREMIER

HOW TO DO A WALKING TOUR

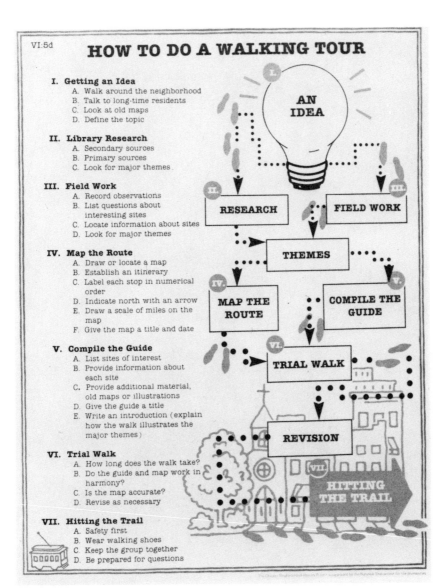

I. Getting an Idea
   A. Walk around the neighborhood
   B. Talk to long-time residents
   C. Look at old maps
   D. Define the topic

II. Library Research
   A. Secondary sources
   B. Primary sources
   C. Look for major themes

III. Field Work
   A. Record observations
   B. List questions about
      interesting sites
   C. Locate information about sites
   D. Look for major themes

IV. Map the Route
   A. Draw or locate a map
   B. Establish an itinerary
   C. Label each stop in numerical
      order
   D. Indicate north with an arrow
   E. Draw a scale of miles on the
      map
   F. Give the map a title and date

V. Compile the Guide
   A. List sites of interest
   B. Provide information about
      each site
   C. Provide additional material,
      old maps or illustrations
   D. Give the guide a title
   E. Write an introduction (explain
      how the walk illustrates the
      major themes)

VI. Trial Walk
   A. How long does the walk take?
   B. Do the guide and map work in
      harmony?
   C. Is the map accurate?
   D. Revise as necessary

VII. Hitting the Trail
   A. Safety first
   B. Wear walking shoes
   C. Keep the group together
   D. Be prepared for questions

Index